THE BIG BOOK
OF CONTENT
MARKETING

THE BIG BOOK
OF CONTENT MARKETING

Use Strategies and SEO Tactics to Build Return-Oriented KPIs for Your Brand's Content

- Andreas Ramos -

Trademarks

Names of companies and products in this document are trademarks, registered trademarks, or trade names of their respective holders, and have been used in an editorial fashion only. Neither infringement, endorsement, nor affiliation is intended.

Disclosure and Promotional Consideration

Promotional consideration wasn't requested nor received.

I'm a co-founder of ClassJunky.com.

for Helen Gong

TABLE OF CONTENTS

Summary of the Book

About the Author

I've worked in Silicon Valley since 1995. I was a technical publications manager at SGI, SUN Microsystems, and over 20 dotcom startups, where I wrote and produced more than 75 printed computer manuals. I co-founded two digital marketing agencies. The second one, Position2.com, got investor funding, opened offices in Palo Alto and Bangalore, grew to 175 employees, and was successfully sold in 2012. I was a director of digital marketing at Acxiom. I'm on the advisory board of six Silicon Valley startups.

I've been writing for a long time. For nearly ten years, I was the National Chair of the Technical Writer Division of the National Writers Union (NWU), where I worked with over 3,000 journalists, technical writers, and book authors.

This is my ninth book. My last three books were published by McGraw-Hill in the United States and Tsinghua University Press in Beijing (Tsinghua is the MIT of China). My books have been published in Denmark, Sweden, Fin-land, Germany, France, the UK, Spain, the United States, China, and Taiwan. Articles by me have been published in an additional twenty-one books, including standard US high school and university history text books and university-level English composition books.

I've spoken at conferences in New York City, Chicago, San Francisco, Los Angeles, San Jose, Phoenix, Beijing, Shanghai, Aarhus, Paris, and Vienna.

As my pro-bono work, I manage the worldwide Google AdWords campaign for MIT's Opencourseware Project (OCW), which is funded by a US$1m Google Foundation Grant. I do this because education enables people to lead better lives, improve the world, and end poverty and war.

I live with my wife and cat in Palo Alto. Visit me at andreas.com.

About the Book

The Book's Advisors

The following people contributed many ideas, joined many discussions, and read versions of the manuscript. I deeply appreciate their help. They're welcome to dinner and the guest room in my house in Palo Alto any time: Alok Vasudeva (Silicon Valley), Bruce Rossiter (Silicon Valley), Cheryl Burgess (Bridgewater, New Jersey), David Broughton (San Francisco), Duane Atkins (Helsinki), Fred Ramos (Palo Alto), Harry Petty (Silicon Valley), Janet Fouts (Silicon Valley), Marianne McGlynn (Denver), Mark Burgess (Bridgewater, New Jersey), Matt Smith (Silicon Valley), Monte Clark (Kansas City), Nan Dawkins (Washington, D.C.), Paul Wistrand (Helsinki), Rob Wynne (Los Angeles), Ronda Broughton (Silicon Valley), Roslyn Layton (Copenhagen), Suzana Gorea (Paris), Wendy Chang (San Francisco)

I also appreciate ideas and postings from people in the discussion groups by the CMPA and the CMA in LinkedIn, and the Facebook group Social Market-ers.

Illustration, Editing, and Production

The editing and production of this book was made possible by a team of people:
- Business strategy by Suzana Gorea of Betwin
- Marketing strategy by Sandra Truc of Betwin
- Content strategy by Mathieu Badie of Betwin
- Project management by Antonin Rémond of Betwin
- Cover, illustrations, and layout by Olivier Sudol of Betwin
- Paris operation management by Claire Scapin and Leslie Lepelletier of Betwin
- Copyediting was supervised by Lisa Carlson and Sydney Pfaff at UC Berkeley Extension. Copyeditors included:
  Alexander Bravo West, Alison Law, Amanda Poulsen Dix, Caitlin Kirkpatrick, Cynthia A. Boardman, Daniel Reyes, Jessica Back, Katie Fox, Marie Oishi, Michael DeLong, Prudence Hull, Robin Goka, Susan Silvius, Sydney Pfaff.
- Soundtrack by
  Lenka, Regina Spektor, Ingrid Michaelson, and Martin Solveig on Pandora.
- Catering by
  Zhihong Gong and Anaximander Katzenjammer.

Printed Book, Digital Book, or eBook?

All of my previous books have been released first as printed books by publishers. However, in the last few years, book publishing changed fundamen-tally. Tablets outsell laptop computers and the number of tablets doubles every year. More than a third of American households now have a tablet. New tools allow digital publishing and distribution.This book will be released primarily for digital distribution. A few hun-dred copies will be printed. See my blog for more about digital publishing.

Why Do I Use Numbered Sections?

This book will be read on laptops, tablets, and smart phones. It'll also be read on paper as a printed book and as printouts. People can adjust the font and line spacing on their mobile devices. If you're reading this as a paperback book and your friend is using a Nook, you can't use page numbers to tell him where to find something in this book. That's why I numbered the sections. No matter how you're seeing this book, you cite and find any section by number.

Dollars: Australian, US, Hong Kong, or Canadian?

When I write $100, which is an actual market price (that's what they charge), then I write US$100 to show that it's US dollars. But if I write $100 without a country label, then it's just an example number. You can think of it as 100 Euros, 100 RMB, or whatever you like. I didn't do this in tables because it looks cluttered.

The Audience for this Book

This book is anyone who uses digital marketing.

Companies, Universities, and Organizations

This book can be used by individuals, companies, government offices, uni-versities, churches, and many kinds of groups, so I use the collective concept of organiza-tions. So when you see "organization," this can be your company, your school, and so on.

Ask Questions. Say Something

Do you have a question? Do you want to say something?
Add your comments at the book's Resources page.

This Book's Resources Page: Updates and Downloads

For updates and free material, go to the book's Resources page at
andreas.com/c-m/

Foreword for the US

I received a call in February of 2010 from the director of my media team in our California office. Search marketing services fell under the media umbrella at the digital agency services that I ran at Acxiom Corporation, and we'd been searching (no pun intended) for months for a heavyweight to head up the search team. "I found the guy", he said to me as I picked up the phone. At that point I was just happy that it looked like we had finally filled the position. He told me the guy he'd found was Andreas Ramos. I did what any good future boss would do and did a search on his name before even hanging up the phone.

I was thunderstruck.

I don't know what amazed me more; that my media director had con-vinced Andreas to join Acxiom or that Andreas himself wanted to come work for us. Because the search results indicated that Andreas Ramos was not merely some guy who had done a little search marketing here and there. No, this guy actually wrote the book on search marketing. (Actually, several books! You should read them.)

Anyway, I had the pleasure of working with Andreas for the next several years. I got him in front of as many clients as possible and used his thought leadership to improve perceptions of the entire digital agency. He's a whipsmart guy who can make complex subjects easily understandable to folks like you and me.

But back to this new book by Andreas. I've written and spoken extensively on a phenomenon I call the new marketing democracy. The pervasive nature of digital channels and devices has given birth to a new world where consumers trust each other more than they trust marketers, they seek to avoid commercial messages until they are in the market for something, and they make their voices heard when a company makes a misstep in the marketplace. For marketers at companies looking to "win elections" in the new marketing democracy, this book is a must read. The label of "content marketing" is thrown around carelessly by many in the marketing profession, without a clear understanding of what exactly it represents. But as Andreas writes in this book, "The proper name for this should be customer-centric marketing, which means for the customers' sake."

In the pages to follow, Andreas takes lessons from all the digital channels and tactics and shows how they can be leveraged to get your customers and prospects the information they need right now in any number of places, engaging them through websites, email, social networks, mobile, blogs – you name it. You'll see again and again how it isn't content that you want to provide, but rather content your customers and prospects want that drive conversions and loyalty.

But you'd be mistaken if you think this book is only about what types of content you can create and where you can place that content. Because Andreas covers a broad range of topics that are essential learnings for those whose job is to generate customer engagement and revenue – topics like remarketing, search marketing, and the metrics that matter when proving to your boss that you are getting the job done.

So get ready. You're about to learn a lot of valuable things. Best of all, you're really going to enjoy reading this book. If you don't agree, I'm sure you'll let me know. Because that's how the marketing democracy works!

-- Chris Marriott
Vice President of Services & Principal Consultant at The Relevancy Group
Chicago

Foreword for Europe

Why should marketers market content? They are paid to market products and/or services!

This is the first question I asked Andreas Ramos when he offered Betwin the chance to sponsor and distribute the « Big Book of Content Marketing » in Europe.

The multiplication of digital channels gives marketers the extraordinary opportunity to measure and predict the behavior of their audience: what kind of information generates engagement, sharing, conversations, etc. for what kind of audience in terms of location, demographics, sociographics and psychographics, for what kind of product and service categories, on what kind of channels.

Andreas Ramos teaches here, in a clear, straightforward way, the techniques, rules and pitfalls to avoid for marketers who discover what content marketing really is about.

Reading Andreas' book helps clarify what makes a successful content strategy.

1. A content marketing strategy is aligned with business objectives as well as branding challenges.

2. A content marketing strategy is measurable i.e. uses metrics (audience, traffic, engagement, content consumption, product consumption) and analytics for a finer customer knowledge.

3. Content marketing is a performance-oriented marketing technique that needs appropriate data expertise, tools and solutions to ultimately drive content propagation to generate audience, boost business and optimize budget allocations.

As we are managing the launch of the book in Europe where we are pretty much focusing on Brand Content, I want to emphasize that despite the difference in naming, Content Marketing is just the best way to put analytical thinking (performance, KPIs, data, business generation, channels planning versus audience, etc.) in the more emotional aspects of Brand Content strategies.

Thank you Andreas for helping us find the optimal compromise between rational and emotional for content strategies!

-- Ariel Ohayon
Founder and Manager, Betwin
Paris, France

Preface

Content marketing is a natural outgrowth of the web's maturity. After an early infatuation with self-indulgent gimmicks, most marketers realized online success depended on giving visitors the information they sought, not pushing a sales message. Soon, the idea "content is king" took root. Content marketing was the inevitable result.

Long before the Internet, savvy marketers produced special interest magazines, recipe books, how-to manuals, and other indirect sales publications to create new uses for their products, stimulate sales of existing lines, and burnish the image of their brands. From this foundation, the Internet has opened a vast new potential for this approach. Moving beyond the printed page, today's content marketing has exploded into a new universe of media and online venues. The opportunities are unprecedented.

In this book, Andreas Ramos delivers fresh insights into the strategy and execution of content marketing based on decades of experience with some of the world's best-known brands. After reading the galleys of the book, I predict it'll become an indispensable resource for marketers across the globe.

-- Ronda Broughton
Principal at AgencyAxis
Silicon Valley

Why Did I Write this Book?

There's a reason I wrote this book. I've been working in marketing for the last ten years. Clients included Fortune 500 companies, Silicon Valley startups, and many small businesses. I saw over and over that as much as 80% of online marketing budgets were wasted (Tim Suther, CMO, Acxiom, 2012) due to poor targeting, wrong messaging, blocking by the audience, and so on.

We often talked about how to improve marketing. That led me to influ-encer marketing. If we could reach the influencers, who are 1% of the audience, the remaining 99% would see our message. Of course, the best way to reach influencers is through content, which led me further to content marketing.

I bought the leading books on content marketing at Amazon and began to read. I noticed some of the books didn't go into details about web technology. I got into marketing from an engineering point of view. I wrote one of the top books on HTML during the dotcom boom. I wrote the code for dozens of websites by hand. I have a great deal of hands-on experience with SEO, PPC, and web analytics. A book on content marketing has to be based on how the underlying technology works and its implications for the business model and the strategy.

I also noticed some of the books don't discuss business or metrics. It's easy to say that you should create lots of content. But how would you know if that works? Without metrics, traditional marketing couldn't prove whether it had any effect on revenues. It's not just metrics: it's how metrics are used. The metrics of traditional marketers weren't aligned with the organization's business goals. I'm on the advisory board for a handful of Silicon Valley startups and I'm often in investor meetings. If a startup doesn't present business oriented metrics, it is ignored by investors. C-level executives and the board underinvest or cut funding for marketers who don't understand business. That's why marketing is often ignored by C-level executives, the board, and investors who underin-vest or cut funding.

When you realize digital content can be combined with automation and tracking, websites can be built that use tailored content to attract the right per-sons and move them along the sales funnel to a purchase. Add email automation, marketing automation, and CRM (customer relation management) and the website turns into software. Add tracking, metrics, and business KPIs. You get a marketing platform that produces measurable results and creates profits and revenues.

A marketing process, based on business goals and objective metrics, can show its contribution to top-line and bottom-line goals. Marketing becomes a manageable investment: Put $100,000 into marketing and get $500,000 in revenue.

Let's make this personal: As a metrics driven marketer, you can compete with sales for bonus and compensation because you can prove that you produced leads and sales. Coffee's for marketers.

Marketing, which has been around for over 100 years, has been energized with many new digital tools. Web 1.0's digitization of text allowed people to distribute content, which undermined traditional content distribution. It also allowed marketers to track activity and results. Web 2.0 added tools to uncover the audience's interests and allow interaction between you and your audience. By adding business processes, marketing automation, and CRM, we can build marketing that works.

1. How We Got Here: Advertising and the Web

1.1.   What's in this Chapter

To understand how content marketing came about and why it's important now, let's take a quick look at the history of media and advertising. It's clear that media is undergoing change. What is driving that change? A collection of new tools are changing production and distribution of content. More tools give the audience new power. Content marketing is built on these changes.

1.2.   The Way It Used to Be: Print, Radio, TV

To understand where we are today, let's see where we came from.

From the earliest civilizations to the beginning of the 1800s, craftsmen and farmers could easily sell whatever they produced. They worked at their own pace, only a few hours a day, and sold mostly to customers whom they knew. Some used small ads, but these were like the flyers that people still put up today in café pin boards.

The Industrial Revolution introduced steam-powered tools and conveyor-belt factories, which allowed companies to produce in vast quantities. A new problem arose: a company had to convince buyers to buy its products (and not the competitors' products). Consumerism, marketing, and advertising are a secondary result of industrialization.

Large-scale distribution of information was created with the Gutenberg press in the 1400s and lasted to recently with little change. For more than 500 years, books and magazines were printed on paper by machines and distributed to book stores and newsstands.

The Industrial Revolution had an impact on the business model of information. As companies needed to promote their products, they looked for ways to reach customers. Companies began to place notices in newspapers. In response, newspapers realized they could charge for this. Nearly all major media today is based on advertising. This started with *La Presse,* a newspaper in Paris, which was the first to base its business model on advertising. Other newspapers had been showing ads since the early 1700s, but advertising wasn't the basis of their business. *La Presse's* sales price was half of other newspapers, so to make up the deficit,

Figure 1: *The first ads appeared in La Presse in Paris, September 15, 1836. As you can see, these ads included insurance, pharmaceuticals, and job placement. We've had more than 176 years of advertising.*

they sold advertising. Other newspapers quickly followed. Radio borrowed this idea in the 1920s. Commercial television followed in the United States in the 1940s. In the mid-90s, Yahoo! hired media executives from New York and Los Angeles, who introduced the methods of mass media advertising to the web. The other major dotcoms quickly followed and they became media companies.

I looked in the national archives in France and found the Sept. 15th, 1836 edition of *La Presse*, which I reproduce in Figure 1.

The combination of industrialized production and placement of advertising in media created a major industry. US$497 billion dollars was spent worldwide on advertising in 2012 (*Ad Age*, Dec. 2012). US$159 billion was spent in the United States. Advertising is growing at several billion per year, so for 2013 it'll be over US$500 billion.

1.3.   The Evolution of Content

Let's look at the impact of the digitization of information and how this created the Internet, Web 1.0, and Web 2.0. Finally, I'll show how that led to content marketing.

First, let's start with what we had before digitization. Up to the mid-90s, information was reproduced mechanically. Books and newspapers were produced with printing presses the size of a locomotive that required skills to operate and maintain. For large-scale reproduction, the process was industrialized, which meant machines, power, and large teams of managers and workers, all of which required large amounts of financial capital.

Distribution was also a physical process. After books were printed, they were shipped on 1,500-pound pallets to bookstores. Books had to be stored in climate-controlled warehouses to prevent humidity damage. This added yet another cost.

Due to historical reasons, publishers could publish only within a country. Kings, religions, and nations kept a strict censorship of books and newspapers to control information. There was no such thing as worldwide book publishing or distribution.

At every step of the way, costs were added to cover salaries and profits.

1.4.   Web 1.0: Digitization of Content, Distribution, and Search

Digitization changed every aspect of the production and distribution of information. In the mid-80s, people began to share digital files and documents by disk or local networks. Soon they were using the Internet to distribute digital files. Digital distribution dropped the price of duplication, storage, and distribution to zero. Today, a book or video is available worldwide instantly. No government or religion can prevent the flow of information.

Starting in the mid-90s and onwards, traditional industries in the production and distribution of books, magazines, newspapers, music, and video have been under relentless assault. They can't compete against digital distribution because they have high production expenses and their distribution systems are slow and difficult. Since they can't enforce their control over production or distribution, publishers switched to enforce legal control over information. The music recording industry hired lawyers and lobbyists to change copyright laws, even to the point of suing people for hundreds of thousands of dollars to scare others from copying music. Book and newspaper publishers have been trying to enforce *all rights contracts* to get all rights to content, including music, movie, musical, theater, video, and game rights in all countries and technologies, including technologies not yet invented and universes not yet discovered. These legal maneuvers are efforts for survival among traditional publishers. However, they can't compete against free. Newspapers, radio stations, and book publishers will disappear as major industries. A few will survive on a small scale, much in the same way you can still buy horse saddles.

The web itself has undergone rapid evolution. In the 1980s, the Internet was plain text. By the mid-90s, images were added to create web pages. Web 1.0 was mostly brochureware, which meant the sites were a duplicate of the company's paper brochure. Soon, developers began to add database capability, which created websites with catalogs of products, order forms, and online payment. Web 1.0 exploded into millions of sites, which required a way to look for something. At first, there was Yahoo!, a simple index of the web. But the web continued to grow, so by the late 90s, better search engines were developed that could quickly index hundreds of millions of pages. Search engines exist because there are lots of pages.

The dotcom boom (which lasted precisely from August 1995 to April 2000) was driven to a large degree by speculation in the stock of websites that had large amounts of traffic. Whether that traffic had any revenue value (or even actually existed) is another discussion. In any case, after the dotcom crash, the focus shifted from traffic to revenues. Investors looked for websites that actually made money, such as Amazon and others which had focused on growing sustainable businesses. Investors suddenly discovered the value of revenue and tracking. There was a demand for revenues-based metrics, so web analytics was developed to track visitors, clicks, cost-per-click, conversions, and cost-per-conversion. That led to Clicktracks, an early web analytics company, and later to Coremetrics, Omniture, and Google Analytics. Google AdWords also became popular because it could track advertising expenditures and sales.

1.5.   Web 2.0: AJAX and the Social Web

HTML was originally developed by physicists in the early 90s so they could publish and distribute their research papers in physics. That's why HTML is so good for building web pages. But the scientists never intended it to be used for shopping and interaction, so it lacked those capabilities.

In the early 2000s, developers began to move beyond HTML. A set of tools, called AJAX , made it possible to build interactive websites that visitors could use. For example, in an old website, a map was just an image and you couldn't do anything to the map. AJAX made the map interactive so you could zoom in or out, add terrain or weather, or grab the map and slide it to see more. AJAX was renamed Web 2.0, which is what we now know as the social web or social media. People could add comments, vote, make changes, and so on. Web 2.0 sites include Google Maps, Facebook, YouTube, and WordPress.

Web 1.0 was the distribution of information. Web 2.0 (the social web) is people talking with their circle of friends. You don't really need search engines for that. In fact, search engines get in the way. If I'm in Paris and want to find a tea house, I'd like one that's the kind that my friends go to. So instead of searching for a tea house, my phone should know that I'm in Paris and suggest to me that my friends like a tea house that's only two blocks away. Google had 7,500 engineers working on their search engine while Facebook had only a dozen engineers for that. Search isn't important to Facebook. People still use search engines when they use their desktop computers to search for information, but for everything else, such as keeping up with friends or looking for tea houses, they use their cell phones and social sites.

1.6.   Web 2.0 Destroys Traditional Media

You'll often hear at conferences that new forms of media don't destroy old forms. The speakers say the new forms take their place alongside the old forms.

That's simply not true. These new forms of media will undermine traditional media because they collapse the production and distribution costs to nearly zero. One person can communicate to a billion people at nearly zero cost. Traditional media can't survive on zero.

- Print is being destroyed because the web allows free distribution of text. Newspaper and magazine revenues are in steep decline. Book publishing and bookstores are in a downward spiral.

- The collapse of the music industry has an odd history. Up to the 80s, you listened to music on the radio or records. In 1981, music changed from an audio-only format into what we now call videos, where music became a soundtrack to the video image. It was easy to move music videos to the web, so YouTube, Vimeo, Vivo, and others became a better way to watch music videos because you can pick what you want to see. MTV, which created the music video in 1981, finally abandoned it in 2008 and has become just another TV channel. Radio music is disappearing because online music sites let you select what you want to hear or you use iPods or cell phones to listen to your music collection. Kids also swap massive amounts of digital music among themselves.

- Broadcast TV will end because video production and distribution is now basically free. A video can be made by a child with her phone and a kitten. The advertising revenue for web-based video is a fraction of broadcast TV revenue. The average CPM for TV advertising in the United States is US$24.68. For web banner ads, CPMs are US$2.66 (that's 11% of TV's CPMs. Forrester Research, 2012). This will be catastrophic because TV is expensive to produce and distribute. It can't survive a 90% cut in revenue.

The traditional distribution of information worked because there was tight control over distribution. Most countries had only two or three TV networks and these stayed within the countries' borders. The only choice for TV viewers was to watch those few channels or turn it off. TV viewers couldn't talk back to the TV. It was top-down one-way broadcast.

Newspapers, radio, and TV didn't realize that the loss of control over distribution would lead to their end. Newspapers earned 30% of their revenues from the local classified ads in the back of the papers. In 1996, I shared a cubicle in Silicon Valley with a guy who was building a website so his high school friends could buy and sell stuff. Late at night, we would talk about his side project, but it never occurred to Craig and me that it would kill the newspaper industry.

Here's where it gets really interesting. When people began to use the web, they slowly began to realize they had freedom to do whatever they wanted. You could read anything you wanted. You could see anything you wanted. You could talk with anyone anywhere. You could copy music, books, video, or photos onto your computer and share with your friends. Whatever your interests, you could quickly find new friends and like-minded communities.

- People began to look for information on their own. Instead of relying on salespeople or marketing, they looked on search engines, asked in forums, read articles by experts, and discussed with friends and family. Suspicious of advertising's one-sided self-interested claims, people researched on their own. People now have completed most of their research and made their decision before they even contact a salesperson. Sales no longer sells; they only take the order. When Stephanie wanted a new car, she collected articles, looked at reviews, and compared information. She compared prices at all dealerships within a 90-mile radius and forced the closest dealer to match the lowest price.

- People began to create. People write blog postings and digital books. People use digital tools to create their books, music, video, and photos and then other tools to distribute those via the web to friends. They do this without talking to traditional services for production or distribution. Justin Bieber was just another kid who was posting his video clips to YouTube. My last eight books were printed and distributed by publishers. With digital publishing, I can do this myself on a scale they can't match.

- People began to share. They wrote reviews, voted up or down, or forwarded information to each other. When I was looking for a new refrigerator, I asked on a social site and a friend told me about Sears Outlet, where I could get a new refrigerator at a 70% discount. Naturally, Sears doesn't advertise this.

The Internet and Web 1.0 created a system for digital distribution. Web 2.0 enabled social communication. The audience can talk with each other. The audience can talk back at the organization. The organization can't control the conversation. Marketing can no longer push a message at the audience. The audience just walks away. Or just clicks away to another site. In a way, the new Chief Marketing Officer of your company is your audience. They decide what they want to hear.

1.7. This Leads to Business-Centric Content Marketing

The combination of digitized information, the Internet, Web 1.0, and Web 2.0 create a new way to distribute information

You use Web 2.0 tools to listen to your audience to understand their concerns. You solve those issues by creating customer-centric content. Web 1.0 lets you reproduce and distribute your content. Use the methods of SEO to make sure people can find your content. Use highly-targeted digital advertising, including banner ads, to let your audience know about your content. All of this can be tracked, which allows testing so you can optimize your content for best results. The key issue is to align your marketing with your organization's business goals. This turns marketing into an investment.

This also means organizations can use the tools of content marketing to bypass traditional content distribution. In the past, organizations had to ask or pay newspapers, magazines, and TV to write about them. Sometimes, the media did this, but usually from their point of view. By using content marketing, organizations are able to manage their own message to their audience.

1.8. Introducing Content Marketing

What am I talking about when I talk about content marketing?

Content marketing is the use of content (text, images, audio, and video) within a larger marketing platform that includes basic marketing concepts, the distribution and search tools of Web 1.0, the social tools of Web 2.0, digital advertising, automation tools, tracking, and business metrics.

Let's unpack that sentence. What does this really mean? How do you use it?

- You listen to your audience to understand their concerns, issues, and problems. You use Web 2.0 tools, including sentiment monitoring, forums, engagement metrics, and so on. You then provide content to solve those issues. This becomes customer-centric content.

- You use the basics of marketing (including branding, a brand style guide, unique value proposition, and an audience) to design the look of the content. Any good book on marketing covers these for you.

- Content has several basic categories: text, images, audio, and video. Each of these categories has formats. For example, text can be FAQs, technical publications, white papers, and so on. Images can be illustrations, photographs, or infographics.

- Web 1.0 collapsed production and distribution costs to nearly zero. You can produce and distribute a book or video for practically nothing. The explosion of websites also created a need for search engines. Content marketing uses the web for distribution, which allows free distribution to reach as many as possible within your audience. Content marketing is based on the public's desire to research on the web and talk with each other before they talk with sales.

- Web 2.0 added AJAX, social media, and social tools. This allows organizations to discover what their audience is talking about. This allows organizations to produce content that is truly appropriate to the audience's needs. You can add Web 2.0 tools to your site to encourage audience interaction and understand what they want.

- Use SEO to make sure your organization's content can be found wherever your audience looks for information.

- Digital advertising allows you to advertise your content to your audience. This can be highly-targeted so you reach only those who are interested in your message. This includes text ads in search engines, banner ads, remarketing, and so on.

- Automation tools, such as email automation, marketing automation (MA) and customer relationship management (CRM), allow you to manage the visitor traffic.

- Tracking tools such as web analytics, funnel analysis, and conversion tracking let you monitor and adjust your campaigns. You use A/B split testing and multivariate testing to find what works. This also allows you to track KPIs.

- Finally, you use business metrics to make sure your marketing is aligned with the organization's business goals, which are measured with top-line and bottom-line metrics. This turns marketing into a measurable investment that can be managed. The data is also objective so anyone can see that it works.

Isn't that easy? You have an overview of everything.

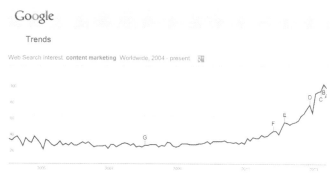

Figure 2: *Interest in content marketing began to grow in early 2011. The graph was created with Google Trends (April 2013).*

Content marketing isn't just creating lots of content. Content is nice. However, knowing what your audience really wants, and delivering it, is better. And even better is when your content helps your organization to achieve its business goals.

1.9. Is Content Marketing New?

There was little interest in content marketing before 2011. Then, in early 2011, searches for the term began to grow (See Figure 2). In 2012, 91% of CMOs were using content marketing and allocating 34% of their budgets to it (Content Marketing Institute, B2B Content Marketing, 2013). Budgets for the creation of content reached US$43.9 billion in 2012 (Content Marketing in America for 2013 by the Custom Content Council).

1.10. What is "Content"?

A common question at events is "what is content?" In general, content is information that people read, view, or hear. But I'm using the word "information" loosely: it can range from technical documentation to sales material to a video, podcast, or a comic book.

There are four major categories for content. Each has various formats.

- **Text:** Annual reports, technical documentation, research, reports, FAQs, white papers, blog postings, enewsletters, books (both digital and printed), ebooks, magazines (both digital and printed), press releases, case studies, social media postings (Facebook, LinkedIn, Twitter, and so on).

- **Images:** Infographics, photographs, PowerPoint slides, drawings, illustrations

- **Video:** Interviews, how-to videos, TV shows, entertainment videos, skits.

- **Audio:** Podcasts, music, sound samples.

1.11. Content Marketing In Contrast to Other Forms of Marketing

Marketing can be divided into two broad categories:

- **Push marketing:** As the name says, you push advertising at your audience. No, this doesn't mean you push your audience away, but that's often what happens. Push marketing is also broadcast marketing, which means you broadcast your message at the audience. There is also interruption marketing, which means you interrupt what the audience is doing. A TV ad interrupts the audience while they're watching a TV show.

- **Pull marketing:** This is marketing that pulls (attracts) the audience. You offer information or hold an event that attracts the audience. Another name is inbound marketing (which means the audience is inbound). Content marketing is a form of pull marketing.

You've probably realized that "content marketing" isn't really the right name for this. It includes the word "marketing," and that implies pushing content at the audience in some way. The best forms of content aren't sales material. People want FAQs, help pages, product specifications, technical documentation, white papers, and comparisons. That's what they seek. The proper name for this should be cus-tomer-centric content, which means it is for the customers' sake. But we're stuck with the label "content marketing". In this book, content marketing combines ideas from Web 1.0, Web 2.0, tracking, and metrics.

1.12. Problems with Current Content Strategies

Many of the current content marketing strategies use only parts of this model.

- Short-term purpose. Organizations create content around an event or product, launch the content, and a few months later, abandon everything, and move to the next campaign.

- Lack of editorial direction. The different teams or divisions produce content on their own. There is no overall editorial direction for the organization's content. That also means lack of consistent branding. This is a common problem at large companies that have bought smaller companies.

- No listening to the audience. The content is presented from the organization's point of view. The organization publishes what it thinks is important. It doesn't use Web 2.0 tools to discover the audience's concerns. It doesn't' look at forums, discussions, votes, sentiment, and so on.

- Lack of metrics. Generally, content doesn't have tracking built into it. For metrics to be useful, the team's overall purpose has to be aligned with the organization's business goals.

- No business goal. Instead, there is a vague hope it'll improve branding or increase awareness.

Some of you are thinking that I'm talking about your company. This is the situation at many organizations. Most organizations continue to use a broadcast model to present content at their audience.

1.13. The Argument against Content Marketing

I've heard a number of reasons against content marketing. The two most common arguments are spam and competitive secrets.

- **Spam**: A lot of content is spam. The authors want to produce as much as possible to overwhelm the search engines and the market space. These articles are created by software (so-called article spinners) or low-skill low-paid workers. Don't worry about this. You should produce high-quality content. Your audience can tell the difference and will choose you.

- **Competitive secrets**: Why should you tell your competitors what you're doing? Won't it just help them? Oddly enough, most competitors don't really compete. For example, there are very good books on how to build a brand, yet most companies don't develop their brand. So most of your competitors won't use your secrets. You're trying to reach your customers, and they can tell the difference between leaders and followers. By standing out, you attract customers.

Think of the top three or four people in your field. They constantly talk about what they're doing by writing articles, books, and blogs. That's what makes them the leaders of your field. They set the agenda and the direction of your field. Because they say what they're doing, others can discuss it. If you want to rise to the top of your field, be open about what you're doing.

Figure 3: *If you black out the advertising on the International Herald Tribune web page, you end up with very little text.*

1.14. The Arguments for Content Marketing

The strongest argument for content marketing is the fact that traditional marketing doesn't work very well anymore.

- People see as many as 5,000 ads per day. They've learned to ignore advertising. The *Financial Times* reported (Aug. 2012) that Unilever spent US$6.3m on TV ads for Axe body spray. The audience was 18-to-24-year-olds, but as many as 60% never saw the ads: they were on the phone, fast-forwarding through the ads, or ignoring the TV altogether. Simulmedia used Nielsen data to show that only around 20% of a TV ad's audience actually sees the TV ad.

- People use online music services such as Pandora and Spotify to get music without advertising.

- 63% of the web users use software to block ads. They also delete cookies (Sequenti.al "Cookies Are Out," Sept. 2012).

Figure 3 gives an example of the *International Herald Tribune* where I blacked out the ads. More than half of the web page is advertising.

Web 1.0 and 2.0 has taught your audience to use the web to learn about products on their own.

- More than 60% of customers decide what they will buy without talking with the sales team (MarketingSherpa, 2012).

- 57% of the purchase decision is completed before the buyer talks with sales. (Jill Rowley, Eloqua)

Your customers contact your sales people only when they're ready to purchase. Marketing is responsible for the sale, not the sales team. The only job left for the sales team is to take the order.

This means you have to meet your audience on their terms. They're looking for information about products and services. Most organizations do a poor job of providing that information. Your organization can give your audience what it wants and you'll get the business.

Content marketing also gives you another advantage by making you an influencer. By producing high-quality content, you become one of the influencers of your market. Instead of being just another competitor, you can be at the top. This means you get a larger share of the market revenues.

Generally, only 1% of the participants in any market are the influencers of that market. This means only a few hundred people are the leaders of their industry. Thought leaders create the direction of their industry. Products rise or disappear when thought leaders point the way. Steve Jobs convinced everyone that the iPod was the next step in portable music, which ended Sony's three decades of domination in that market.

You can also use content marketing as an aggressive competitive strategy in your market space. By producing the leading content in your category, you gain a visibility in the market place. Your audience will notice your organization, wherever they look. With a clear branding strategy, your organization will build recognition among your audience.

The search engines give preference to quality content. Content sites, blogs, tweets, and others will also include your content. This means your organization builds a visible presence in the search engines and the web, which means higher ranking and more visibility. This also becomes a strong barrier to entry and a significant competitive advantage.

This certainly doesn't mean you should create lots of filler content. Try to produce the best-in-class content.

Leroy Merlin is a French brand that provides home improvement solutions tailored to each customer's specific need. Leroy
Merlin created the first sponsored TV program in France 25 years
ago. Called Du côté de chez vous ("around your home"), it shows
how ordinary people carry out home improvement. Leroy Merlin
launched a print magazine that is sold in bookstores and newsstands. The clever idea was to create a magazine as a distribution
channel which is now marketed as an independent product.

1.15. Summary of this Chapter

There are two key factors in this chapter. Traditional advertising was based
on traditional media's mode of production and distribution. Web 1.0's near-zero
costs for reproduction and delivery destroyed traditional media. Web 2.0 enabled
the audience to research on its own and talk among themselves. With the end of
traditional media, broadcast advertising as we have known it will end.

2. The Basics of Marketing

2.1.   What's in this Chapter

The point of this quick chapter is to show how content marketing fits into the larger framework of marketing. To create good content, you first prepare the groundwork. Good content uses the business goals, branding, and messaging. It's created with the avvvudience and sales funnel in mind.

2.2.   What's Your Business Goal?

A business goal tells you what you want to achieve. You develop strategies and tactics to reach that goal. It also lets you know which strategies and tactics can be ignored because they won't help you with that goal.

The goal should be aligned with your company's overall business goal. The CEO, the CFO, and the board are generally clear about the goal. Find out what the company's goal is and then develop your goal to work within that goal. This means you start at the end.

State your goal as a number and a date. This lets you measure progress towards that goal. For example, your goal is to increase revenue by 15% by December 31st. You will increase market share by 10% by the end of the second quarter. You will increase leads to 500 per month. You will lower cost-per-lead to $50 CPL in four weeks. You will shorten the sales cycle by 20% in six months. You will cut costs by 10% within a year.

A business goal isn't a mission statement ("To do the best for our shareholders") or a code of ethics ("Be honest."). Those statements don't support the business goals, give you targets, or set deadlines.

It sounds obvious you should know where you're going. But I've joined many projects where this wasn't clear. The project had been set up years ago and the original team had left. By then, the project had gone though several generations of teams. Nobody really knew anymore why things were being done the way they were. This is a widespread problem at large Silicon Valley companies, where workers tend to move every two years.

Another problem is the fog of internal politics. If upper management is wrapped up in bureaucratic wars, they forget to manage the divisions so there are no goals or metrics. Teams are left on their own. Without guidance, there are no goals.

I was working with a VP of a small company several years ago. I asked her for a copy of their branding guideline. "We haven't gotten around to writing that." Who are your target customers? "Whoever buys our stuff." So what is your cost-per-lead? "We don't really know how to calculate that." I got a bit frustrated and asked so what's the marketing plan? She said "We just sell as much as we can." Hey, that works. A few years later, they sold the company for US$50 million.

2.3.   Develop Your Brand

A key concept in branding is *salience* , which means something stands out from the others in its category. An organization can make its brand stand out from competitors by developing a distinctive and memorable logo, colors, fonts, packaging, and messaging. Make it easy for your audience to notice, recognize, and recall your organization, your products, and your ads.

Salience can be passive or active. Passive salience is when people recognize your brand when they see it among other brands. If I go to the store and see Colgate on the toothpaste shelf, I recognize the brand. However, if my shopping list reminds me to buy toothpaste and I think of Colgate before I've even entered the store, that's active salience. I've already selected the brand and I won't consider competitors.

You increase your brand's salience by using a consistent look for all of your content. You always use the same colors, fonts, and layout in your documents and videos.

You also increase salience by being ubiquitous in all channels. Your audience will see your brand and content, wherever they look. This means a strong advertising strategy to appear in search engines, social media sites, and online magazines for both desktop and mobile devices. Use SEO, text ads, banner ads, and so on. This also includes offline channels, such as TV, magazines, and so on. The more people see your brand, the more familiar it becomes, which also increases their favorable attitude towards your brand. Repetition makes your brand appear safer and accepted.

This brings us to the *brand guideline* . This is a short document that tells your team how to use your brand elements. You create a brand guideline document and distribute it to anyone who creates content for you. It allows anyone to create additional documents that match your organization's content.

The Big Book of Content Marketing | Andreas Ramos

The brand guideline includes:

- Where to find the current version of the brand guideline
- Who is in charge of the brand guideline
- Creation date (when the current document was created)
- Expiration date (when the document expires, which prompts the reader to look for the current version)
- The purpose of the organization
- The audience
- Where to download the logo in various sizes (a small logo for email signatures, a medium logo for websites, a large logo for posters, and a very large logo for cloth banners)
- Specifications for the colors (e.g., HTML #CA0000)
- The fonts, style, and size (e.g., body text in Palatino 10 points)
- How to write the URL, such as ClassJunky.com
- Location of the image library
- Location of the Model Release Form (for photography and video)
- Guidelines for voice, tone, and images to use (and avoid), including punctuation
- Sample documents in Word, PowerPoint, spreadsheets, letterhead, and so on

The brand guideline should be a practical document that any of your creators (writers, photographers, videographers, and so on) can use when creating content.

A brand design has to work in various displays, including cell phone screens, desktop monitors, letterheads and business cards, cloth banners at events, and more. If you're delivering products in boxes, the branding has to work with the box, the product, and even how the product comes out of the box. Carefully open a new box from Apple and notice how they manage the presentation. The different kinds of paper stock also affect how people perceive your brand. A brand guideline should be designed by someone who has training and experience in this.

Most companies don't understand the importance of branding. Go to your supermarket and look at the tea section. Some of the packages stand out because they have distinctive logos, colors, and fonts. The packaging also matches the product. It tells you what the company thinks of its tea. For example, some companies now offer tea in metal containers with air-tight caps. You can tell this will seal the tea's freshness and aroma. Other tea packaging is just a plain box where the logo is often hard to see. Those companies don't put effort into branding, so they don't stand out. Look at the different supermarket aisles and you'll see that most products have poor branding. The ones with good branding generally are the leaders in their markets.

Develop a branding guideline and get everyone to use it to create content. This improves the salience of your brand, organization, products, and services.

My book is an example of brand design. The overall appearance of the book was developed by a graphics person. The illustrations match the cover's style. The colors also match, both inside and outside the book. The layout is also consistent with the book's graphics. In contrast, illustrations in most books are random. There is no attention to style or branding.

I placed an example of a branding guideline at the Resources page, along with a collection of corporate brand guidelines.

2.4. Your Brand Statement

The brand statement is what an organization wants to say to its audience. That sounds easy enough, but the brand statement is often a challenge for organizations. Whether they're new or established, it's very hard for them to state their message.

- Organizations are self-centered. They see the world (both customers and competitors) from their point of view. It's very hard to step outside and see your own organization from the customer's point of view.

- The more loyal and enthusiastic you are about your organization, the harder it becomes to see it from other points of view.

- The more you know about your organization, the more unique it seems to you. You know the purpose and details of your products and your competitors and the differences are clear. But outsiders generally don't see that.

These factors make it difficult to write the company's brand messaging. The result is usually complex and overloaded with political and bureaucratic baggage.

- Brand statements are also called unique value proposition (UVP), unique value statement (UVS), brand value statement, or similar.

- There are a few rough rules for writing your brand message:

- Say it in three words. Can you reduce your organization's history, thousands of employees, and hundreds of products to just three words?

- Spoken, not written. It should sound natural when you say it.

Your Chinese grandmother. Yes, your Chinese grandmother should understand what your organization does. Back in the 90s, we called this the Mom Test. Software should be so simple that even a mom could install it. But now, most Palo Alto moms have a Ph.D. in engineering. So we can use Chinese grandmothers until they start to get Ph.D.s.

These three rules are a good start to writing your brand message. Think of the global brands: Just do it. Thank heaven for 7-11. You're in good hands. World's biggest bookstore.

2.5.   Your Audience

One of the key steps in a marketing strategy is to define your audience. People often assume they should advertise to as many as possible, but that's not feasible. There are 502 million people in the European Union. Obviously, it would be expensive to advertise to all of them when only a few will buy your products or services. So you look for the people who will are most likely to buy.

A simple way to target is by geographic distance. If you have a store, look at your customer records and if you find your furthest customer lives 44 kilometers away, then you only need to advertise within that radius. Many stores use this method to determine where they will show their newspaper ads and flyers.

If you're reaching a nationwide audience, you can target by demographics. Data marketing companies such as Acxiom use demographic data such as income, age, sex, location, and education to sort the population into groups. For example, Acxiom sorted the US population into 71 socioeconomic clusters. Each cluster has between two to five million people. People within those clusters have similar backgrounds and behaviors. These clusters have numbers and names, such as "#62, Kids & Rent," which is made up of parents in their 30s and 40s with children of all ages. Primarily high school educated, they're employed in technical, clerical, and craftsman jobs. They're a mix of Caucasian, African-American and Hispanic families. They're almost all renters. They invest in their children. Their pastimes include movies, video games and sports. The cluster report includes detailed data on the types of financial services they use, where they shop, what they watch on TV, the magazines they read, what they do for fun, and the sites they visit on the web.

Acxiom has 1,500 types of data for everyone in North America, Europe, the Arab world, and Asia. For example, they know the kind of car that you drive, when you bought it, how you paid for it, and the color. By knowing the behavior of the other five million people in your cluster, they can predict when you'll buy your

CASE STUDY: MAGGI

Maggi is a Swiss company that makes bouillons, soups, seasonings, noodles and sauces. The company was started in 1884 to provide low-cost food. Most of their products are condiments to be added to other foods, so their UVP is "bring out the best in every meal." They build a content marketing strategy by publishing recipes that Maggi products can enhance. They also encourage creativity and ask bloggers to create recipes that use their products. They also sponsored chefs who went to homes and helped families to prepare meals with Maggi products.

COMMUNICATION & CONTESTS ON NEW PRODUCTS, RECIPES, AND COOKING CULTURE *

OFFICIAL CHANNEL: SHORT PROGRAMS FEATURING RECIPES, CHEF TIPS, AND ADS.

VIDEOS ARE DUPLICATED ON LOCALLY RELEVANT PLATFORMS

MAGGI'S CUSTOMERS

PARTNERSHIP WITH A POPULAR NON-PROFESSIONNAL COOKING BLOG; ITS AUTHOR DEVELOPPED RECIPES AROUND MAGGI PRODUCTS

THE WEBSITE PRESENTS THE PRODUCTS, RECIPES, IDEAS OF MEALS WITH MAGGI'S PRODUCTS, AND SOME DISCOUNTS

* POSTS EVALUATED ON NUMBER OF LIKES, SHARES, AND RETWEET

next car, what kind of car you will buy, and even your color preference. Since they also know which magazines you read, what TV shows you watch, and the websites that you visit, they can place advertising to reach you at the right time.

These companies also know your street address, your phone number, and the six different IDs that you use at various social media sites. This lets them reach you with digital ads wherever you look. Since they know your street address, they can also target by zip code. A fascinating field is *geodemographics*, which means people in the same cluster also tend to live in the same area. Researchers have identified the clusters for each of the 45,000 zip codes in the US. This means if Honda knows the clusters for its audience, then it can advertise precisely in the 652 zip codes where cluster #62 lives and not waste money by advertising in zip codes with clusters who won't buy that particular car.

By knowing the audience and cluster, you can write a media plan. This lets you know where to place content and advertising so it'll be seen by your audience (and where to not place advertising which won't been seen). A media plan includes magazines, TV shows, and websites. If you know they read *American Baby*, then you can place articles in the magazine, along with advertising. A cluster analysis also lets you know what interests your audience. This lets you create content that helps them to make decisions for their lives and families.

Your audience is more than a simple buyer profile. You find not only that they read *American Baby*, you also find out their financial capability (whether they can buy your products), their media consumption habits, and their address for targeted mailing, both postal and digital.

If your organization is small, you can create a profile of your audience by other means. One way is to carry out a poll of your subscriber list. You don't need to ask all 20,000 people or whatever you have in your list. It's enough to ask only 2,400 people in order to get responses with a ± 2% margin of confidence. Use PollCode. com or similar to create a free poll. Ask the questions that you'd like to know and send it to a random selection of 2,400 customers. You can ask for their job titles. See if you can understand their motivation to purchase. Ask them why they buy from you. You can also ask why they don't buy from you. Is it price? Service? Ask what they want to get them to buy from you.

Another way to create an audience is to look at the business roles of people that are likely to be your customers. I worked on a project last year where the audience was companies between US$50 million to US$250 million in annual revenues and in three certain markets. I then looked at who was the decision-maker in those companies to determine their job titles. I used business directories and LinkedIn to come up with a list of 600 people by job title, name of company, and contact information.

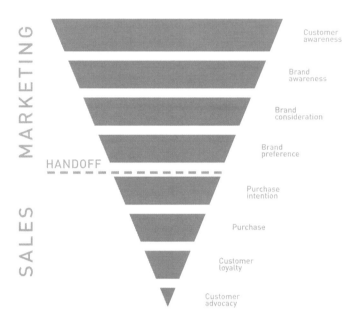

THE BUYING FUNNEL
KOTLER & AL.(2006)

Figure 4: *The buying funnel (also known as the purchase funnel, buying cycle, purchase cycle, and so on) was first described by Elias St. Elmo Lewis in 1898. Philip Kotler's Marketing Management made it a standard concept in marketing.*

Let's look closer at your audience. It's obvious your audience can be divided into two parts: the ones who haven't yet bought and the ones who have bought. That's useful because we can focus our marketing at the ones who haven't yet bought.

We can separate them into further groups.
- People who need your solutions, but don't yet know about you.
- People who are comparing solutions and suppliers
- People who decided to buy from you and are looking for the best price and delivery

Your customers go through several phases in the process to becoming your customer. Some researchers have identified three phases; others have added more phases, such as awareness, interest, desire, action, and loyalty (post-purchase behavior). In this book, I'll use the basic model of three phases (awareness, consideration, purchase). You can adapt what I say to your preferred model.Because the number of people in the audience becomes smaller and smaller as they move through the phases, a funnel metaphor is often used.

This matters in content marketing because you create different kinds of content, based on the phase of the buyer:

- **Awareness**: Your buyer is vaguely aware of a problem, but don't yet know what to do. "Does this matter?" "What's going to happen?" "What will it cost if I don't fix this?" You can offer information about the consequences of the problem.

- **Consideration**: When the buyer realizes he has to fix it, he begins to consider solutions. "What can I do about this?" "What are my options?" You can offer information to explain options and possibilities.

- **Purchase**: The buyer decides what he has to buy. New kinds of information can explain the cost-of-ownership, price and feature comparison with competitors, payment options, and additional issues.

The content at the different phases shouldn't be mixed up. Someone who is only just becoming aware of a problem isn't ready to look at pricing and purchase options. He first needs to learn about the problem.

Some writers argue that the buying funnel isn't relevant anymore with the Internet. It's certainly true that for many products, there isn't a buying funnel. The web makes it easy to make an instant purchase of a song or download an app. American consumers switch from instant purchase to evaluation at somewhere around US$300. They began to compare features and prices. The purchase of home products for long-term use, such as refrigerators, can take months. In nearly all B2B purchase decisions, the buying funnel can take up to six months or longer and involve different teams at each phase. You will have to create content to support decision-making at each phase and to move the customer forward to the next phase. This means the buying funnel, in whatever form you use it, will be a fundamental part of your content strategy.

2.7.   Understand Your Competitors' Content Strategy

Make a list of your top three-to-five competitors. For each of these, answer the following questions:
- What are their business goals?
- What is their content strategy?
- What is their brand strategy?
- Who is their audience?
- What is their advertising strategy?
- What are their problems?

Are there opportunities for you? For example, if they're weak in a key audience, can you go after that group?

Every six months, do a quick review of your top competitors to see if they have made any changes in their strategy.

2.8.   Use Content Marketing as a Barrier-to-Entry

You create a barrier-to-entry to make it difficult for your competitors to participate in your market. By placing real or perceived difficulties in their path, your competitors fall behind. Content marketing can play a role in keeping your competitors out of the market. Here are several things that you can do:

- **Technology:** Digital publishing isn't easy. There are many kinds of tools, formats, and distribution channels. The more tools you use, the greater the challenge for your competitors to keep up. Don't rest by using only a few tools. Use as many as you can.

- **Presence:** By creating a body of valuable content, your audience sees your organization wherever they look. This puts your competition in your shadow.

- **Continual innovation:** Digital publishing is also evolving rapidly. New tools and platforms appear every few months. We're doing things today that didn't even exist two years ago, and you can be sure there will be new possibilities in two years. By constantly innovating, you stay ahead of competitors. Most of them take the easy way and relax. Every six months, make a review of the field and add new technologies.

- **Hire your competitors' key people:** Find out who they are and bring them over to your team.

2.9.   The Creative Brief

Similar to the brand guideline, the *creative brief* is a document that ensures consistency in the production of content.

The creative brief is a short one-page document that states the terms and conditions for production and delivery of work. Sometimes, the agency sends a questionnaire to the client and other times, the client sends a statement to the agency. Either side can deliver this. It states:
- Where to find the branding guideline
- Name and contact information for the project manager
- Project ID
- Delivery deadlines
- Description of the project
- File formats
- How to deliver the work

The point of the creative brief is to set expectations so the team can easily create and deliver work with a consistent quality and format.

There is also a sample creative brief at the Resources page.

2.10.   Recommended Reading

Marketing is fascinating because it is at the intersection of human behavior, business, technology, and finance. Here are several books for further reading:

Marketing Management, by Philip Kotler (14th ed., 2011, Prentice Hall). This is the world's most widely-used graduate textbook in marketing. To understand marketing as professionals see it, read this. Philip Kotler teaches at Kellogg at Northwestern.

Brand Relevance, by David Aaker (Jossey-Bass, 2011). Considered the foremost expert on branding, this book shows you how to become the leading brand in your market. It includes dozens of case studies on how to use branding to create opportunities for you and threats for your competitors. Professor Aaker teaches at UC Berkeley Haas School of Business.

Designing Brand Identity, by Alina Wheeler (4th edition, 2012, Wiley). She lays out a five-phase process for creating an effective brand identity. Includes 30 case studies.

How Brands Grow, by Byron Sharp (Oxford University Press, USA 2010). Fascinating metrics-based analysis of thousands of companies and markets to explore how brands grow and die. He's a professor of marketing science at the University of South Australia and the director of the Ehrenberg-Bass Institute for Marketing Science.

The New Strategic Brand Management: Advanced Insights and Strategic Thinking, by Jean-Noël Kapferer (Kogan Page, 5th ed., 2012). He's Europe's leading authority on brands, and internationally acknowledged as one of the most influential experts on brand management. A Professor of Marketing Strategy at HEC Graduate School of Management in France, he holds a PhD from Northwestern University.

Who Cares Wins (Why Good Business Is Better Business), by David Jones (FT Press, 2011). This is a brilliant book from the CEO of Havas which demonstrates the importance of the coherence of a company's message and its real practices.

Brand Content, by Daniel Bô (Dunod, 2009, in French). This is the reference book in France on the concept of content marketing. This book was awarded the 2009 *Grand Prix des Études* Silver Award. Daniel Bô holds a degree from HEC Graduate School of Management in France.

2.11. Summary of this Chapter

For content marketing to be done well, it has to be in the context of the elements of marketing. You have to do the groundwork of setting business goals, branding, messaging, audience, and the buying funnel. With a solid foundation in place, you can build a content marketing strategy.

3. Creating Your Content

3.1. What's in this Chapter

Content marketing is a collection of ideas, strategies, and tactics. It includes the team, a set of business ideas, and various tactics. In this chapter, we'll go through these to see how they're assembled together.

3.2. The Elements of Content Marketing

Let's dive in. There are a number of elements to content marketing. Let's first list these and then go through each one.

- **Managing Editor:** The managing editor guides overall operations, maintains the voice, sets the level of quality, and gets the content out on time.

- **Content Team:** The team includes writers, illustrators, and videographers. It also includes people to manage the development of content, such as developmental editors, copyeditors, and quality control. There are also community managers and support staff.

- **Alignment with Business Goals:** The marketing strategy is aligned with the organization's business goals. This is measured with top-line and bottom-line metrics.

- **Buying Funnel:** The content move the visitor from one phase to the next of the buying funnel: awareness, consideration, and purchase.

- **Branding:** All content fits within a unified branding strategy for consistent look-and-feel. This includes a standard logo, colors, fonts, layout, and voice. The audience can recognize the organization.

- **The Audience's Concerns:** Use Web 2.0 tools to understand your audience's concerns and issues. The content should address those concerns.

- **Metrics:** Every item has tracking to show the number of views, leads, conversions, and similar.

- **Testing:** Use A/B split testing and multivariate testing tools to evaluate and improve performance. Weak items can be removed.

- **Editorial Calendar:** list of all content items, the purpose and roles for the content, who does the work, edit/release dates, art work, tags, tracking codes, and more. A complete editorial calendar can have 60 or more columns and list tens of thousands of content items.

- **Serial Publication:** Content isn't produced as a one-time event (for example, monographs). The content is produced as part of a series on a schedule. This motivates the audience to return repeatedly.

- **Purpose of Item:** Every content item has a call-to-action (CTA). This moves the visitor to the next phase of the buying funnel. Every item contributes towards achieving the business goals.

3.3.   The Managing Editor

A number of people use the idea of a small town newspaper as a model for an organization's content marketing strategy. For decades, the small-town newspaper was the center of its community. It acted as a common space where people shared news, and talked about issues. Announcements were made of births, weddings, and funerals. These newspapers learned to listen closely and write about the issues that mattered to the community.

Newspapers have a publisher, who oversees both content and business; the editor-in-chief, who oversees the operation, including hiring, budgets, and so on; and the managing editor, who oversees the content itself, including delivery, voice, and quality.

Your organization's content strategy must have a managing editor. This person leads the strategy and ties everything together.

The managing editor:
- Has a sense of what the audience wants
- Writes for the audience
- Sets the voice and style
- Maintains the quality level
- Act as a referee to the community discussion
- Manages the team and process
- Supervises everything

The managing editor is a public role. The audience should know who the managing editor is and how to reach him.

Depending on the size of your company, you may have several people in different roles, or a few people with multiple roles.

The managing editor builds and manages a content marketing team. This may include the following roles:

- **Managing Editor:** The managing editor sets the voice and style, maintains the level of quality, manages the team and process, supervises everything, and makes final decisions.

- **Your Audience:** The audience has to be considered as part of the team. You're writing for the audience. You have to be aware of what the audience wants. Use an array of Web 2.0 tool to do this. You also use tracking tools to gauge their response.

- **Developmental Editor:** The developmental editor plans the organization of the content, selects categories and formats, edits headings and outlines, rewrites, restructures content, deletes con-tent to improve flow, and identifies gaps in content.

- **Copyeditor:** The copyeditor checks voice, clarity, spelling, grammar, punctuation, capitalization, list numbering, illustration labeling, subject-verb agreement, and consistency. She also removes wordiness, triteness, convoluted text, and inappropriate jargon. She checks the content against the style manual. Copyeditors are critical for producing quality.

- **Quality Editors:** The quality editors ensure the content lives up to brand guideline. They review final content and either approve it or send it back for further development or editing.

- **Writers:** The writers produce articles, FAQs, white papers, ebooks, and more. They interview SMEs (subject matter experts), senior staff, key people in the industry, and customers. If you hire outside bloggers, look for people with followers. You should be posting twice a day or more.

- **Graphics Team:** Trained graphics people produce illustrations, in-fographics, layout for text and web pages, and so on.

- **Video Team:** The videographers create video. This includes inter-views, product demonstrations, weekly shows, and webcasts.

- **Community Managers:** The community manager monitors the social media accounts, such as LinkedIn, Twitter, Facebook, and so on, plus the comment boxes at your website. Community manager tools include Tweetdeck, HootSuite, Sees-mic, SproutSocial, and Sprinklr. She also watches the web for mentions of your organization. She responds to comments. If it's useful, she thanks the contributor. If someone has a valid complaint (something doesn't work), she acknowledges the problem and forwards it to the right person. Some people make negative comments. Cite the terms of use and block their comment.

- **Support Staff:** Carry out distribution of the content by placing items on various sites, including Facebook, Twitter, YouTube, and so on.

3.5. Web 2.0 and Your Audience

One of the differences between content marketing and other forms of marketing is the use of Web 2.0. In other forms of media distribution, especially traditional media, the content was distributed as a broadcast at a passive audience, which was one-to-many and top-down messaging. TV news, for example, was broadcast at the audience.

Web 2.0 bypasses this model of distribution. The members of the audience use the web and social tools to talk, discuss, and organize among themselves. Organizations have learned the hard way that they can't censor or delete these discussions; the audience simply moves out of reach to a site where the organization has no control. Heavy-handed attempts to control a conversation can also provoke a backlash.

Your organization's best approach is to join the game. This means your organization becomes a participant in the conversation. Your organization may play a larger role than the audience in that your team is creating the bulk of content, but you're still a participant in the conversation. People will comment, discuss, share, edit, and distribute your content.

Oddly enough, after nearly ten years of Web 2.0 and social media, the social tools still aren't very good. An ideal Web 2.0 platform would allow people to place content in a secure repository for sharing, allow collaborative editing, and distribute the edited content. Currently, Wendy can upload her images, but I can't edit them in her account and add my new version to her account. I can't upload my photos into her account. Privacy and security almost don't exist. We don't yet have tools that deliver the promise of Web 2.0.

Use Web 2.0 tools to learn the audience's concerns in order to produce content that appeals to them:

- **Sentiment:** Use sentiment monitors to evaluate the general sentiment (positive, neutral, negative).

- **Feedback:** Encourage the audience to give feedback. Collect and review all feedback. Hold a weekly staff review meeting, where comments, feedback, and so on are reviewed and discussed. Use their issues to create content items.

- **Ratings:** Encourage the audience to rate some items. Use this to see what is popular or not.

- **Likes and follows:** The number of likes and follows also indicates interest.

- **Comments:** Encourage the audience to add comments. The audience engages in conversation among themselves. Collect and review the comments to find issues where you can create content items.

- **Mentions of your brand and products on other sites:** Use monitor tools to see if your organization, products, or services are mentioned in other sites. Monitor the sentiment and trend of those mentions. Your community manager should interact with those comments.

- **Modify your content**: Allow your audience to modify and share your content.

- **Create content**: Create a space at your website where you release content for others to edit. This can include FAQs, videos, music, and so on.

There are several ways to find topics:

- Look at the social question-and-answer sites where people ask questions and others answer. Questions are sorted by categories, so you can find a large pool of questions to see what people are thinking about. Yahoo! Answers (answers.yahoo.com) is visited by over 100 million people every month. Additional question sites include Answers.com (38 million), Answerbag, askville.amazon.com, AllExperts, JustAnswer (7.5 million), theanswerbank.co.uk, and Quora.

- Search for topics in Twitter. Scroll back six months, copy all of the postings, and review those.

- Collect questions from your sales and support team. They know the "top ten" questions that customers ask.

- Put a prominent "Ask us a question" box at your website and collect the questions.

- Look at the blogs and Twitter feeds of experts and influencers.

- Look at your website's search box. If configured correctly, your web analytics makes a list of all queries.

Go through all of these questions. Assign the questions to writers. Post the question to your blog or web page as the title and write a reply. Answer these in FAQs, web pages, and so on.

For example, at Quora, I searched for "content marketing" and found 384 questions. I printed these out and found 41 useful questions for this book, my blog, and Twitter.

3.6.   The Goal for Each Item of Content

Traditional marketing was generally a series of short-term campaigns. Sometimes, the content had call-to-actions which told readers where to go for more information, but often it didn't. When the campaign ended, the content was generally abandoned.

Content marketing is a long-term project. Ideally, the items are never abandoned.

- **Branding:** The content item uses clear branding to build awareness and salience.

- **Answer the visitor's concerns:** The content item answers the person's question at that step of the buying funnel.

- **Motivate to the next phase (Call-to-Action):** The question is answered and the next question is raised. This moves the reader to the next step of the buying funnel. Every content item should end with a strong call-to-action which can be a button or link that prompts the viewer to the next step. Instead of a general "Read More" button, try buttons or links with clear information. "Compare our tea filters with competitors." "What is the cost of ownership?" "What other options do I have?" "Order today and get free shipping." Try different texts and see what works best. If you use buttons, try different colors and compare the results.

- **Tracking:** Tracking lets you know how many people viewed the item in that phase of the buying funnel and how many went forward to the next step in the buying funnel. The tracking also lets you see the item's contribution to business metrics: did it contribute to a lead or sale? How much revenue was produced?

- **Serial publication:** The content item is part of a serial publication.

As I wrote above, there are four general categories for content. Each category has formats:

- **Text:** Annual reports, technical documentation, research, reports, FAQs, white papers, blog postings, enewsletters, books (both digital and printed), ebooks, magazines (both digital and printed), press releases, case studies, social media postings (Facebook, LinkedIn, Twitter, and so on).

- **Images:** Infographics, photographs, PowerPoint slides, drawings, illustrations

- **Video:** Interviews, how-to videos, TV shows, entertainment videos, skits.

- **Audio:** Podcasts, music, sound samples.

I include everything so you have a restaurant menu where you can see what's available and you can pick what is appropriate to your project.

Use your data to see which categories and formats are relevant to your audience. Don't rule out a format because you're not familiar with it. Use data to justify your decision.

Be careful with polls that show what other marketers are using. I have several of those polls, but I won't put them in this book. As you already know, 80% of marketers don't use data. A recent poll stated 38% of marketers believe infographics are effective. If they don't use data, how would they know if it's effective? Without data, there is no objective basis for those polls.

It's not feasible to include a list of distribution sites for each item. For example, there are over 250 video distribution sites similar to YouTube. These change constantly. Use as many distribution sites as you can.

Use an editorial calendar to manage the production of content. The editorial calendar can cover:

- **Project calendar:** An ID for each item, along with start dates, delivery dates, and other deadlines

- **Content inventory:** The types of content, the audience, the title, goals for each item, and other details

Adience's Concern	Format	Mgr	Author	Art	Budget	Due	Post	SEO	Goal	Metrics
What will happen if I don't fix this?	FAQ	Helen	Haiyan	Megan	$200	June 12	Blog	Metatags	Go to sideration page	Number of views
What are my options?	Comparison	Zhihong	Naxi	Megan	$250	June 18	Blog	Metatags	Go to product features page	Views, Leads
What's the benefit?	Customer	Helen	Emily	Magan	$175	June 26	Blog	Metatags	Go to customer testimonials page	Views, Leads

Table 1: *Editorial calendar example.*

- **Technical details:** Keywords, URLs, tags, and tracking information

- **Team assignment:** The managing editor, writer, videographer, copyeditor, quality editor, and so on

- **Metrics:** Clicks, leads, sales, cost-per-lead, cost-per-action, and more

- **Recurring events:** Weekly, monthly, quarterly, and annual events, holidays, product release dates, conferences, organization events

Your editorial calendar can be simple or complex. It should fit your organization and projects at your level. This can start as a simple spreadsheet and evolve from there.

Your editorial calendar should be available to people on your team so they can check their assignments and update the calendar. This could be set up in a collaboration tool that allows sharing and group editing, such as Microsoft Office 365 or a Google Docs spreadsheet.

In general, the editorial calendar supports the three phases of the buying funnel (if you use a different model for the buying funnel, adjust it to that). This means the first section covers the awareness phase; the second and third sections cover the consideration and purchase phases.

Break down every part of the awareness phase into columns. Start with the basics and add columns as you grow. The basic columns include the audience's concerns, the topic, who will do the work, delivery dates, and basic metrics.

You can download an editorial calendar at the book's Resources page.

Your audience has different intentions at each phase of the buying funnel. They're looking for different types of information. Here are suggestions for types of information for each phase of the buying funnel:

Awareness:

- The Audience's Intention: In the awareness phase, they're learning about the problem.

- Type of Information (Formats): Show the problem. Explain why it's a problem. Show what could happen if it isn't solved. Items include FAQs, white papers, customer stories, videos. You can also include material that shows your thought leadership in your industry.

Consideration:

- The Audience's Intention: In the consideration phase, they're learning about the solutions. They're evaluating their options, so they look for comparative information that compares the vendors, solutions and products.

- Type of Information (Formats): Describe solution options. Compare your solution against your competitors. Items include FAQ, industry analyst reports, white papers, competitive comparisons, cost comparisons, cost-of-ownership information, installation videos, benefits, and opportunity for training, technical specifications, technical documentation, awards and industry recognition, collection of press articles about your product or service, and access to your community.

Purchase:

- The Audience's Intention: In the purchase phase, they've decided to buy your product. They're learning about their options for purchase, so they're looking for pricing, payment, delivery, service, and so on.

- Type of Information (Formats): Show how to buy and install. This includes pricing, payment plans, delivery, installation, service and support options, training, technical documentation, updates, and support information.

Create pages for the phases of the buying funnel and place relevant information on those pages. Use advertising to bring a broad audience to your initial pages. From those opening pages, you add subsequent pages which move the visitor to the next phase. By answering the initial question, you bring up additional issues.

You tell your visitor that she can get the answer to those new questions by clicking the link to move to the next page. These call-to-action (CTA) links also let you track the traffic.

You shouldn't mix these up. Someone who is just becoming aware of a problem isn't interested in options for payments over 24 months. At best, he'll ignore that. At worse, he'll look for another website with the information that he wants and never return.

By creating decision trees, you can separate and segment your audience into different categories. For example, to separate customers into large or small companies, offer two documents, one for companies with several offices and another for companies with a single office. Get a clear understanding of the categories of your customers, and create content items that help you to segment your audience by letting them move to the type of information that they want.

3.10. Email Automation and Email Newsletters

One of the most effective forms of reaching your audience is through an email newsletter. Although email is often seen as old-fashioned, it has the highest click-rate and has the lowest cost-per-lead of any form of digital marketing because your readers chose to subscribe to it. They can also easily unsubscribe, so if someone's on your email newsletter list, she wants to hear from you.

Use email automation to build your email list. These tools let you put a subscribe form or link on your website. Your subscriber list is maintained as a spreadsheet. When you create an email newsletter, it can automatically insert first name, last name, and city (for example, "Dear [Laura] in [San Francisco].") You can also separate your list in segments based on interests, so an investor firm can send emails where there is a paragraph for investors who are interested in petrochemicals and a different paragraph for investors who are interested in biotechnology.

The email automation tool will report the results. It can show that you sent out 10,000 emails; 2,000 were bad addresses (the email is no longer active); 8,000 were delivered; 6,000 opened; and 4,000 clicked.

There are a number of email automation services and tools. At the enterprise level, there is Acxiom, Experian, Responsys, and others. For small operations, MailChimp starts with a free service that lets you send up to 20,000 emails per month. These tools let you create emails with your branding and logo.

After you send out an email, you can reuse the content by posting it to your blog, Twitter, and other social sites. Put a copy in your newsletter archives at your website so search engines can index it.

3.11. Technical Documentation

You may notice technical documentation in the list of formats. Technical documentation (also called tech docs, technical publications, or tech pubs) is rarely mentioned in content marketing. I think it's ignored because many people in content marketing come from sales and marketing, not the tech pubs team. However, one of the best forms of content is documentation because its intention is to inform the reader.

If your organization has a technical publications team, you should include them in your content marketing strategy. Look at what they're producing and see how you can increase its visibility. You'll find customers prefer to look at technical documentation, not marketing material.

Technical manuals play a key role in sales and marketing. When I was the director of tech pubs at Brio (a database company later bought by Oracle), I went on sales calls as a technical sales support and saw that prospects wanted to understand the product before they bought it (it was fairly complex software) so I gave them the manuals. I did print runs of 25,000 manuals, so there were plenty of manuals. The sales team began to hand out manuals, both print and PDF, to prospects and leads. One day, a sales guy called me from the back of an airplane. He was on a flight from NYC to Los Angeles and was sitting next to the VP of company who became interested in Brio. The VP wanted a manual. I called the Kinko's near the airport and sent them a PDF of the manual which they printed and delivered to the airport.

3.12. Books: Printed or Digital?

Although digital books get lots of attention at the moment, you get much more credibility when you hand someone a printed book.

You can use print-on-demand (POD) to produce printed books. This can be as low as US$2.93 per book. You can use POD to print both hardback and paperback books. I have hardback and paperback POD books and the production quality is equal to books from large publishers. Amazon Create Space is a widely-used POD service.

However, in general, the layout of POD books is generally done by non-professionals, which explains the poor appearance of the text. That is why it is important to work with professionals for copyediting and layout of your material. You don't want your company to be perceived as cheap or worst, nonprofessional, do you?

What does this mean to have book publisher? My last two books were published by McGraw-Hill. At the time (2009), the large bookstores (Borders, Barnes & Noble, and so on) only carried books by large publishers, so I sent a book proposal to ten large publishers who didn't have books on the subject. Three accepted. McGraw-Hill made the best offer, plus their office for technical books is in San Francisco (about 45 minutes from Palo Alto), so I chose them. McGraw-Hill as the publisher gave the book strong credibility, which led Tsinghua University (the MIT of China) to publish the Chinese edition.

As the author, I can buy books at bulk price, so I bought cases of books to give to prospects and clients. The book was basically a "one-pound business card." People also saw the book in the large bookstores and contacted me for services. The 10% royalties were insignificant. The secondary income, such as speaker fees and clients, were greater.

I distinguish between ebooks and digital books:

- **Ebooks** are generally short (perhaps 50-75 pages), have lots of colorful graphics, and are meant as sales material. The copyediting, index, or graphics was generally not done by professionals. It's unlikely that a large publisher would accept or publish an ebook. The content and structure of ebooks generally don't have the same quality as a textbook by Wiley or McGraw-Hill.

- **Digital books** have the same quality as a professional book, but they're distributed digitally. They have the same attention to layout, copyediting, illustrations, front material, indexing, and so on as books by the major publishers.

I realize these differences may matter only to professionals in the book industry. I describe them anyway so you'll know.

I chose digital distribution for this book. Few people buy business or technical books in bookstores anymore. Borders, which once had nearly 20,000 employees and 700 bookstores, no longer exists. Independent books are rapidly disappearing. The best way to reach my audience is with a digital book. I can give away digital copies of the book because production and shipping costs are zero. I can also distribute a digital book worldwide, which is difficult with a printed book.

There are a number of books on digital publishing. Guy Kawasaki's *APE: How to Publish a Book* (Nononia Press, 2012) is a quick overview. A better resource is Carla King's *Self-Publishing Boot Camp Guide for Authors* (SelfPubBootCamp.com, 2nd ed., 2012). Carla has written seven books and teaches courses on self-publishing. Her book explains the options for producing and distributing your book. Her book was my roadmap for the distribution strategy for this book. I will also release an ebook (yes, a short book) on how I wrote this book (sign up for my newsletter to be notified).

3.13. Monographs versus Serialization

If you ask a professor what she's working on, she may reply she's writing a monograph. That's an academic way of saying that she's writing a book.

To professors and most literary writers, books are written as stand-alone items. The book isn't part of a series. My previous eight books were monographs. Some had URLs and websites, but there wasn't a connection between the books.

In contrast, many publications are produced in serial format. This means they're part of an on-going series. Magazines, comic books, and so on are serials.

Serial publication has a long history. Charles Dickens published *The Pickwick Papers* as the first serial novel in 1836. He wrote a new chapter every two weeks. Readers paid by the chapter. Within a few years, most leading writers were publishing their novels in serial format in magazines and newspapers.

Serialization has several advantages. Once the readers begin to follow the story, they return for the next installment. This creates an audience that returns again and again. It also locks in the audience; if they're following a series, they won't follow others. The newspaper and magazine is able to create a stable recurring audience, which they can offer to advertisers.

Here are several examples of serials in various formats. Some of these serials have lasted for decades:

- **Newspapers:** Many newspaper features have appeared daily for decades: Peanuts (50 years), Family Circus (53 years), Dear Abby (57 years)

- **Magazines:** Magazines appear weekly, bi-weekly, or monthly for decades. Harpers (1850), TIME (1923), New Yorker (1925)

- **TV:** Meet the Press has been on the air for 65 years. Soap operas have existed for nearly 60 years.

- **Radio:** The Shadow, a detective show, lasted 24 years as a weekly series.

- **Movies:** James Bond has appeared in twelve novels and 23 movies over 50 years.

- **Events:** The Super Bowl is held yearly and the Olympics and World Cup are every four years

- **Products:** Every Christmas, Hallmark releases a new Star Wars spacecraft as a tree ornament for collectors. Car makers regularly update their cars. Apple has iPhone 1, 2, 3, 4, 5…

- **Software:** It's also possible to serialize software. Windows has appeared as version 1.0, 2.0, 3.0, 98, and XP.

How can you use serialization?

- **Text:** Books, research, reports, white papers, annual reports, slideware, and case studies: State that the item is part of an ongoing series and add a list of other titles. Let your readers know where they can find more documents. Add numbers so people can collect and organize these. For example, IBM 2014, 2015, and so on.

- **Events (both in-person and webinars): Present** these as a series. The same host presents each event.

- **Videos and audio:** they should have a continuity of characters and themes. For example, the same people should host the videos. Open and close the video with your organization's logo and branding. Release these on a regular schedule.

- **Infographics and illustrations:** Add a text box to say that the infographic is part of an ongoing series and tell people where to go for more infographics.

- **Tweets:** they can appear at 9am every day for the start of the day with a heading, such as "Breakfast Tweet."

- **Blogs are a good example of serial publication.** Add blog postings every few days and your readers will follow you. For example, Signe blogs about journalism every Monday. This gives her a writing deadline. Her readers come to expect her postings.

3.14. Where to Find Writers

There are lots of places to find good writers:

- Magazines and newspapers are shutting down, which means an opportunity to hire experienced editors, copyeditors, journalists, and production staff. Look at the leading trade journals for your industry. You can contact the editors and journalists and hire them as staff or contract. Very often, they'll ghost write for you.

- Look at the authors of books in your field. The authors nearly always have a website. Go to Amazon, search for your top keyword, buy four or five books, see which ones you like, and contact the authors.

- Additional resources include BlogDash, Blogmutt, Business2Blogger.com, Contently, eCopyWriters, Docstoc.com, MediaPiston, MyBlogGuest, Zerys

Writers generally specialize by industry, such as legal, telecommunications, biotech, and so on.

3.15. Ghost Writers

If your CEO wants a blog, but she doesn't have time to write, you can hire ghost writers. He writes articles which are published under the CEO's name. Ghost writers don't mind because they're paid for that. Many of the articles that you see in business magazines or the presentations at conferences were written by ghost writers.

Be careful with ghost writers. It's like those movies where the parents are bugging the poor guy to get married and he comes home with a fake girlfriend. What happens when the VP gives a talk at a conference that was written by a writer and someone asks a complex question? Or the ghost gets a better offer from your competitor? Or he decides to go trekking in Bhutan (no email) for six months? (Note to self: Write a movie script with Will Ferrell as the CEO and Kelly Kapoor as his ghost writer. Send to Roger at Warner).

3.16. Quality or Quantity?

For any topic, there are hundreds of articles. Only a few are excellent. You must produce excellent material or nobody will read it.

It is better to produce a few items that are the best in your field, instead of hundreds of average items. People will share the best items among their friends. Nobody shares average stuff.

A good source of content is your own organization's experts. They know their profession, the skills, and the products. They talk to other professionals. Hire a few writers or journalists, either as staff or contractors, and have them interview your experts on a regular schedule.

3.17. Use PR to Place Content

Public relations agencies, in contrast to advertising agencies, promote organizations or individuals by placing stories in newspapers, magazines TV programs, and websites. These are articles, not advertisement.

PR agents and advertising agencies share the same goals: promoting clients and making them seem as successful, honest, important, exciting, or relevant as possible. But the paths to creating awareness are different. Most people understand advertising is paid by the organization and is generally viewed with skepticism. However, when PR agents are able to place articles in respected publications or get TV appearances for their clients, it is generally viewed more favorably because of the perception of third-party validation.

The Public Relations Society of America defines public relations as:

- Anticipating, analyzing and interpreting public opinion, attitudes and issues that might impact, for good or ill, the operations and plans of the organization.

- Counseling management at all levels in the organization with regard to policy decisions, courses of action and communication, taking into account their public ramifications and the organization's social or citizenship responsibilities.

- Researching, conducting and evaluating, on a continuing basis, programs of action and communication to achieve the informed public understanding necessary to the success of an organization's aims. These may include marketing; financial; fund raising; employee, community or government relations; and other programs.

- Planning and implementing the organization's efforts to influence or change public policy. Setting objectives, planning, budgeting, recruiting and training staff, developing facilities — in short, managing the resources needed to perform all of the above.

That's a good overview of the general functions of a public relations agency. The tactics include some or all of the following:

- Write and distribute press releases locally, nationally and internationally

- Speech writing

- Write pitches (which are less formal than press releases) about an organization and send them directly to journalists

- Create and execute special events designed for public outreach and media relations

- Conduct market research on the organization's messaging

- Develop business contacts via personal networking or attendance and sponsoring at events

- Copy writing and blogging for the web (internal or external sites)

- Crisis public relations strategies

- Social media promotions and responses to negative opinions online

Organizations and individuals should hire a public relations agency when they want to protect, enhance, or build their reputations through the media. A good agency or PR practitioner can analyze the organization, find the positive messages and translate those messages into positive media stories. When the news is bad, an agency can formulate the best response and mitigate the damage.

Effective publicists have great relationships with journalists in many different industries. Many PR pros are former journalists, so they know the best ways to pitch a story and reach editors and reporters. Since they aren't employees of the firm that hires them, they can give an outsider view and potential story ideas.

The relationship between organizations and the PR agency shouldn't be passive. Organizations should inform the agency what messages they would like to promote and make suggestions on where they would like to appear. Very few stories make the front page of the New York Times, but with a media atmosphere that includes blogs, websites, TV shows, magazines, and other media that evolves every day, a good PR agency will help organizations increase their visibility via increased recognition on as many respected editorial platforms as possible. Long term, public relations can be an investment in the brand and the visibility of an organization or individual that results in increased recognition and reputation.

You can use automated web services to broadcast your press release. But that won't have much effect, if any. You can see that you need the personal connections of PR agencies to place your content in reputable newspapers, magazines, TV, and their websites.

3.18. A Content Audit of Your Current Material

One of the first things in setting up a content marketing process is to decide if you will carry out a content audit. A content audit is a review of your existing content.

There are two possibilities:

- You make a list of the various content items in your organization. You review your current content, find out what you have, what's working, and what's not working. You also make a list of the various tracking tools, tags, and cookies. Of course, you also sketch out the buying funnel and how the audience should be moving through it. You can also identify if something is missing so you can create content for it.

- You realize the size of the mess and quietly move forward. What's the point of cataloging hundreds obsolete and abandoned campaigns and their bygone content items? There can be tens of thousands of pages, articles, documents, videos, and images. At any moderately-sized organization, this can run into the millions of items, especially if there are items or campaigns that are more than ten years old. It can take months to do this. When you finish, you'll then have to go back to rewrite that content and fix all of those tags. The authors of that material are likely gone. It'll probably be more cost-effective to start with a clean field.

Look at your web analytics and see if there are items that still bring significant traffic that converts into leads. Cisco's bunny video might still bring lots of traffic, but if the server is obsolete, you can drop it.

When there was lots of attention to web analytics and we switched platforms every few years, there was often a concern to be able to move data from the old platform to the new one. But after a while, everyone realized old data wasn't useful. Everything changed so much that you couldn't compare today's data with data from even a several years ago.

3.19. How Many Content Items? Think Big. How Big? Real Big.

You're starting to think, wait, this could get big. Tens of thousands of articles?

As I said, many sites think they have a large site if they have 100 articles. But that's because they're still thinking of their website as the center of their distribution model.

My personal site andreas.com has some 350 public pages, along with more than 1,800 photos. There are also hidden folders for friends and family. There are fourteen years of blog postings. All in all, there are over 5,000 files at andreas.com. This is just my personal site. Your organization has a budget and staff, so you should easily have 10-20,000 items.

Zappos has 40 people on the video team, who produce 30-50,000 videos per year. Lynda.com, which offers 1,500 online courses, has 83,000 videos. Udemy has 80,000 videos.

IBM may have the most advanced social media strategy of any large company. Every one of their 433,000 employees has a personal page, which includes space for a blog. 26,000 employees are blogging. They've also arranged themselves in 91,000 communities and posted 623,000 files, which have 9.5 million downloads. IBM employees also share information on 62,000 wikis. They send around 50 million instant messages daily (slightly more than your average teenage daughter). IBM encourages their staff to be on social media sites where they share information, so there are 200,000 IBM employees on Facebook, 295,000 on LinkedIn, and 35,000 on Twitter. IBM encourages their staff to actively distribute and participate, which creates an overwhelming digital presence (See *The Social Employee*, by Mark Burgess and Cheryl Burgess, McGraw-Hill 2013).

Start thinking on how you will produce a body of content with a plan for the next three years. By building a marketing system where you can show success in business goals, you'll get the budget for that. Look at hiring dozens of writers, video, photographers, artists, and voice talents as staff or contractors. Hire people around the planet: there are excellent writers in India, video editors in the Ukraine, artists in China, and voice talents in South America.

This also means you should blog two or three times a day. Hubspot wondered about how often they should blog, so they began to post more frequently. They found the more they posted, the more audience they got. They now post up to five times a day.

This definitely doesn't mean you should spew out content. Some content marketers are using low-paid people or software to create thousands of articles. After they've released thousands of mediocre articles, they can't delete those. Poor content hurts their brand and credibility.

You can maintain a high quality of content. Look at material from IBM, Hitachi, Samsung, and other global corporations. Their content is excellent. Give copies of your branding guideline, creative brief, and sample documents to your team of content creators. All content should be reviewed by copyeditors and quality-control editors. Include tracking on all content. Monitor content by results; if someone is producing content that doesn't reach the average traffic or results, let the person know so they can improve. You can find an example of a branding guideline, creative brief, and more at the book's Resources page.

3.20. Low Traffic Builds Up

What about low-traffic pages? Should you keep those? Let's assume you have a page with only 10 visits per month. That's 120 per year. In three years, that's 360 visits. How much would it cost to get 360 visits by advertising in Google AdWords? If you're paying (let's say) $2 cost-per-click, you'd have to pay $720 to get that traffic. Or you can just leave that page on your site and get the same amount of traffic for free.

But don't just create lots of pages. Make sure those low-traffic pages are useful. They should be a step in the buying funnel and include a call-to-action to motivate the reader to go to the next step.

A few dozen high-quality pages are better than thousands of blah-blah pages. Junk pages will damage your organization's reputation.

Low traffic adds up. I looked at a company that has 66 videos at YouTube. Here are the number of views for each video: 1,023, 1,184, 1,284, 1,410, 108, 115, 130, 131, 132, 139, 146, 146, 170, 176, 2,370, 2,391, 2,451, 2,749, 210, 216, 223, 235, 249, 269, 272, 289, 293, 3,279, 311, 318, 351, 359, 368, 4,336, 40, 408, 433, 436, 445, 483, 488, 521, 536, 549, 567, 572, 575, 579, 595, 597, 605, 641, 645, 680, 695, 713, 715, 742, 758, 788, 810, 824, 826, 839, 857, 98.

None of these videos had large numbers of viewer. However, if we add them together, the company has 46,893 views. If the cost-per-click is $2, it'll cost $94,000 to get that traffic. Those videos will continue to attract visitors without any further investment.

3.21. The Use of Marketing Automation in Content Marketing

A basic tool in content marketing is marketing automation. Marketing automation tools turn the buying funnel from a chart into a tool.

- Use messages to identify the visitor's phase in the buying funnel

- Send the visitor to the appropriate page that has content for that phase of the buying funnel

- Use an offer of further information to motivate the visitor to move to the next phase

- By looking at the visitor's behavior (the pages he visited, the content he viewed, the path, the length of time), you can score the quality of the leads

- You can see which content items worked or didn't work

One of the major problems in lead generation is the lack of follow-up on leads. For all sorts of reasons, as much as 80% of leads are ignored (Forrester, 2012). By using automation, every lead gets attention. Eloqua writes that the use of marketing automation can produce seven times as many leads with twice as many conversions. Hubspot, Forrester, and others report similar results.

If you're competent with HTML, web-based forms, and email automation, you can build your own marketing automation. Define the buying funnel, identify your audience's needs, and create content for each phase. Design a series of pages with decision points to move the visitors into different paths, such as large companies or small companies, personal use or corporate purchase, and so on. Offer content for download which also requires signing up for an email newsletter. You can use VerticalResponse or MailChimp to set up auto-reply email such as "Dear Helen, I wanted to let you know we just published a new white paper "Metrics for Content Marketing." It's not publicly available on our website, but here is a link to it: example.com/downloads/metrics.html, Sincerely, Emily."

The other solution is to have consultants design and install a marketing automation solution. Many small consulting teams offer this. For large companies, solutions include Eloqua, Marketo, or Act-On. For SMB (small and medium business), a well-known solution is Hubspot. SOHO and small organizations can try LoopFuse, which has a free version and can be quickly installed.

Marketing automation is a solution in a self-service website, where the visitor makes his choices and moves through the decision tree on his own. The process is handled entirely by software. Marketing automation is well-suited for a business that has no sales people.

If your sales process ends with turning the customer over to a sales team, then an additional solution is Customer Relationship Management (CRM). CRM tools manage and supervise the sales team by allocating leads to salespeople (based on territory, size of client, etc.), tracking the sales person's response (initial call within 24 hours, follow-up calls, and notes at each step), and results (number of leads, number of sales, quotas, monthly amounts, forecasts, and so on).

The best-known CRM is Salesforce.com. Other CRM tools include Act!, Amdocs, Highrise, InfusionSoft, Microsoft, NetSuite, Oracle, SFDC, SAP, Siebel (now Oracle), SugarCRM, and ZoHo. There is also Pivot-It.com, which offers a free version.

3.22. Which Should I Use? Blogs, Facebook, Twitter, or LinkedIn?

Blogs, Facebook, LinkedIn, or Twitter: which should you use? The real question is whether your audience will be able to find your postings.

Anyone can see any posting that you made today in your blog or Twitter. There are no privacy settings in those.

People can also use any search engine to find whatever you posted to your blog or Twitter a year ago. The search engines index those postings and show them. I searched for blog postings that I made fourteen years ago and tweets from four years ago. They showed up in the search engines.

However, people can see your postings in Facebook or LinkedIn only if you choose to give them access. If you posted to LinkedIn or Facebook groups and the group is available only to members, others can't find your postings.

So if you want your postings to be available to your audience, use blogs and Twitter as your first line of distribution. If you want, you can post to Facebook and LinkedIn as well.

I'll admit it: for several years, Facebook was my primary social site. I've now switched to my blog and Twitter.

3.23. Creating Content for Global Distribution

If your organization has an international presence, several more issues come up.

- **Write in international English:** This is English with standard grammar. People should be able to understand your text if English is their second (or third) language. Don't use examples or metaphors from sports, politics, or religion.

- **Translation into other languages:** Generally, you can use English as the global language. Most multinational corporations conduct their business and internal communication in English. If you're selling to consumers and the market is significant for you, consider translation into that language.

3.24. Examples of Content Marketing

Here are a few examples of content marketing at various companies. There isn't yet a standard approach to this (there isn't even a name for this), so companies have unique solutions. If your organization is offering information to its audience, post your URL at the book's Resources site.

3.25. Intel.com's Focus on Content

Intel's website is a library of information. You should go to the site and see how they make it easy to find documentation. There are categories for products, audiences, and types of content. The Intel website is built around the idea of content marketing as the distribution of documentation.

3.26. Eloqua's Website for Topliners

Eloqua has a community hub for the people who use their software. Topliners is supervised by Heather Foeh as the Editorial Director. She supervises the conversation, adds content, and keeps the site informative. In contrast to the Intel and Citrix sites, the site features a person as the managing editor.

Figure 5: *Go to Intel.com and you'll see their focus on content marketing.*

Figure 6: *Topliners.Eloqua.com, is a content site for Eloqua's community of users.*

Figure 7: *Topliners.Eloqua.com, is a content site for Eloqua's community of users.*

3.27. SDNCentral.com

Matt Palmer and Roy Chua noticed it was hard to find information about software-defined networks (SDN). They used a Twitter feed to develop a following among professionals, executives, and developers. They launched SDNCentral.com as a network hub for the SDN industry. It has lists of organizations, projects, technologies, use cases, events, jobs, blogs, and newsletters. Within a year, they had a LinkedIn group with 1,000 members, 30,000 Twitter followers, and a website with 50,000 monthly visitors. This is another example of an information portal that has people at the center.

3.28. More Examples of Content Portals

As you can see, these sites differ from each other. Each was built as a solution to the company's situation. It's hard to find these because there isn't a name for this yet. Harley-Davidson has HDTalking.com for motorcycle owners. Proctor & Gamble sponsors BeingGirl.com, a site for teenage girls. American Express has OpenForum.com, which offers resources for business owners, such as videos, articles, blogs, podcasts, and expert advice.

If you find interesting examples of content marketing, or you're building this at your company, post to my book's Resources page so others can see what you're doing.

3.29. Summary of this Chapter

This chapter covered many of the elements of content marketing: teams, Web 2.0, goals, formats, editorial calendar, and enewsletters. From all of this, pick what you can feasibly implement in your organization.

4. The Hub-and-Spoke Model of Content

4.1.   What's in this Chapter

Now that you saw the elements of content marketing in the last chapter, let's step back and look at the Big Picture. How do these pieces fit together? What is the relation between your website, the content, the distribution sites, and your audience?

4.2.   Hub-and-Spoke as a Model for Your Website and Content

A widely-used idea in content marketing is the hub-and-spoke concept. Like a bicycle wheel with a hub in the center and spokes which radiate outwards, the website is the hub in the center, where the content originates. The content is then pushed out to the spokes, which are the distribution sites (such as YouTube, Facebook, LinkedIn, and so on). People discover the content at those sites which leads them back to the website at the hub. The company's website is the center of their strategy.

The hub-and-spoke model comes from the transportation and distribution industry. Delta Airlines started using a hub-and-spoke model in 1955. They chose Atlanta as the center (the hub) and all flights radiated as spokes to and from the hub. It's also used by Wal-Mart, which has a hub in Arkansas. The FedEx hub is in Memphis, Tennessee and UPS has a hub in Louisville, Kentucky. (Why these cities? They're in the center of the population of North America.)

The idea of a website or blog as the hub and distribution of content to the spokes is a key concept in books such as *Content Rules*, by Ann Handley and C.C. Chapman (p. 143), *Inbound Marketing*, by Brian Halligan and Dharmesh Shah (p. 12-13), *Valuable Content Marketing*, by Sonja Jefferson and Sharon Tanton (p. 52-53), *Content Strategy*, by Kristina Halvorson and Melissa Rach (p. 77), and *Optimize*, by Lee Odden (p. 109-112). Many more blogs and articles use the hub-and-spoke model for content marketing.

This idea has been widely adopted by websites. I've built hundreds of websites since 1995 and I also used this idea. After much discussion with the book's advisory team and delivering many presentations on content marketing, I began to realize something was wrong.

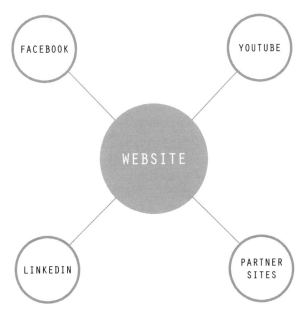

Figure 8: *In the hub-and-spoke model for content marketing, the website is at the center. The spokes point out to the distribution sites where the content is placed.*

Twenty years ago, websites started as brochureware, which means they presented the organization from the organization's point of view. "We have a big office building; we have a CEO; we have a dog." Remember those?

The problem with those sites was that visitors didn't really care about the building, the CEO, or the dog. Visitors wanted to solve their problems. If the website didn't offer the solution, visitors just pressed backspace, returned to the search engine, and looked for another site.

Not much has changed. Today, most websites are basically interactive brochureware, which means they added features such as comments, downloads, registration forms, shopping carts, and so on, but the organization is still at the center. Marketers, web designers, and SEO focus on the organization's website as if the rest of the web doesn't exist. Amazon, for example, is all about Amazon. Facebook would be happy if the rest of the web got deleted.

Now, why is that wrong?

The model is wrong because it doesn't match what's really going on.

You've heard the story of the hardware store and the hammer, right? Nobody goes to a hardware store just to walk around in a hardware store. Nobody really wants a hammer either. Michelle buys a hammer because she wants to put in a nail to hang up a photo of her family. Her desire is to see the photo on the wall; the hammer is just part of the solution. She doesn't care about the hardware store, its CEO, or the dog.

Some of you may wonder what this has to do with a website. Ronda has a website, so she puts her content on her website. So isn't her website at the center? That's where Ronda is making a mistake. If she thinks of her website as the central point of her marketing, then she'll pay attention to her site and she won't think much about other sites. She may add some content to YouTube, Facebook, and a few more, but not much more.

And that's what's going on at nearly every website. Ask Ronda how many items of content she created. Many sites consider themselves to be big if they have 100-200 items on their site.

Next, ask her how many sites she uses for distribution. Probably not more than six.

How should this be different? Ronghua, who has a tea export company in Sichuan, wants to reach as many customers as possible, so she sees her website as *just another distribution site*. Ronghua will also create as much content as possible. Her 500 articles and videos may end up on 2,000 web pages at other sites, because she wants to get the maximum distribution for her content. That gives her more exposure to her audience.

See? You need to think of distributing your content, not controlling it.

So what should be at the center of your strategy?

Your customers should be in the center. The content should be written for them.

- The central issue is *your customers' concerns and their problems*, not your organization.

- Content is information that you create *for your audience and customers*.

- Distribution is how you distribute that content to your audience. You place your customer-centric content on many websites, including YouTube, Facebook, LinkedIn, and, along with all of these websites, your content is also on your website. Your website or blog is *just another distribution point*. When you're successful at content distribution, your 5,000 items may appear on 50,000 pages, and most of those sites aren't yours.

Figure 9: *An improved hub-and-spoke model for content marketing. The audience is in the center. The spokes point to distribution sites where content is placed. Your website is just another distribution site for your content.*

It's actually against your interests to keep your content only on your site. It reduces your exposure to your audience. You want your content to be distributed as widely as possible. You want your ebook not just on your one web page. You want your ebook on 20,000 web pages. Are people copying it and making it available on their websites? Great! The more they share, the greater your presence, which also means greater share of presence over your competitors.

I'm not being flippant. A number of people downloaded my KPI ebook and hand it out to their visitors. Some people uploaded it to various ebook distribution sites. People had uploaded it to six different accounts at one book distribution site. Over 25,000 people had read it. I didn't get a penny in royalties. Was it piracy? Yes. Did I mind? Yes, of course. But the point of my ebook was to show people how to calculate KPIs, so that worked. I wrote the ebook several years ago, when I didn't know about content marketing, so the ebook wasn't trackable. I've fixed that now. If people want to distribute it, that's good.

Widespread distribution isn't just an idea for websites. In Silicon Valley, there's the Red Rock Café. It's a great local coffee house where musicians play music, they show movies, groups meet there, and artists display their work on the walls. But Red Rock is just one café. And then there's Starbucks. Their coffee is available in tens of thousands of supermarkets, millions of hotel rooms, on thousands of pas-

Figure 10: *With the audience is at the center, content is pushed out to the distribution sites. Those content items can be in four different categories: text, images, video, and audio.*

senger airplanes, and many more locations. What's the difference between Red Rock Café and Starbucks? Most websites are like the Red Rock Café: they offer lots of things and interaction… at their website. They haven't moved to the Starbucks model where the customer's desire is the center. Starbucks solves this by ubiquitous distribution. Starbucks' goal is to be wherever people want to drink coffee.

This isn't a new idea. Companies have known for decades that a key factor of success in sales is a large number of distribution points. The more distribution, the greater the sales. Build as much distribution as possible so your content shows up wherever people have the needs that your products and services can solve.

4.3. Put the Audience at the Center of the Hub and Spoke

The audience at the center is a major shift in how to understand web distribution. Just as Copernicus changed the world from a geocentric to a heliocentric model of the universe, we move from a focus on the website as the center to a view where the customer is the center and our website is just another page.

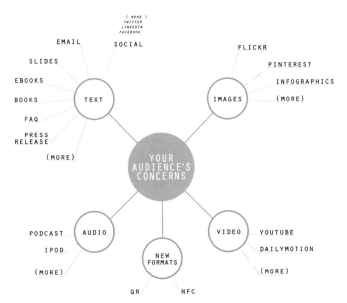

Figure 11: *Each of the four categories (text, images, video, and audio) has formats. Images for example can be infographics, photographs, drawings, and cartoons. Each of these is placed on their appropriate distribution platform.*

This breaks the search engine model of the web. When Megan uses a search engine, she gets a search results page. The search engine shows only ten websites. She won't see all of the other websites for that search.

If your organization has several pages with the same content, the search engine won't show those pages. Megan won't be able to see your additional pages.

This is good for people who are searching in a search engine.

But this hurts your content distribution. Search engines aren't good for your organization's outreach. The search engines have become, for better or worse, the gate to the web. As we all know, the lucky two or three at the top of page one in a search engine get 90% of all the traffic to that topic. Everyone else gets nothing.

You want your content to be available on as many sites and pages as possible. People will discover you on those sites; they will pass your links and content to each other; they will talk about your content among themselves. Search engines don't matter to any of this.

As you'll see in the chapter on SEO, Google isn't the main resource for people to research your topics. You need an SEO strategy that gets around search engines, which we'll cover in that chapter.

For example, you find that your audience wants to know how tea should be brewed (it's not as easy as you think). You reply by writing an article about brewing tea; you make a video; you take a series of photos and so on.

Next, you push the content items to the various distribution sites. For example, the photo essays are placed on Flickr, Picasa, and Pinterest. The videos go to YouTube, Vimeo, and so on. And yes, the articles, videos, and photos also go on your website. Your website is just another distribution point (okay, okay, you can call it your favorite distribution point).

This doesn't mean you must use every format and distribution point. Some formats may not be relevant to you, so you can ignore those. Many distribution sites won't be relevant either, so don't bother with those.

Some of the spokes are sub-spokes. For example, text is the category which leads to the formats of social posting, such as tweets, Facebook, and so on.

Some spokes are longer than others. The ones that are important to you should be closer to your hub. Blogs and Twitter should be close to the center. If you're not doing much video, put it further away.

There are also new formats. QR codes (those funny little dotted squares) and NFC tags may become big. Or not. For some of you, these could be very useful.

For others, not at all. (See this book's Resources page to learn more about NFC).

As I've said before, don't ignore a format or distribution site just because you don't like it. Test it and use data to make a decision. If the data shows it doesn't work, you'll be happy because you were right. If it works, you'll be happy too, because you're getting good results.

4.4.   The Content Engine as a Flow Diagram

While making more than three dozen presentations on content marketing, I realized the hub-and-spoke metaphor wasn't the best way to explain content marketing. In fact, it just raised questions and created more confusion.

It made more sense to explain content production as a linear process that develops ideas into content. The process moves from left to right. The starting point is your audience. The end point is also your audience.

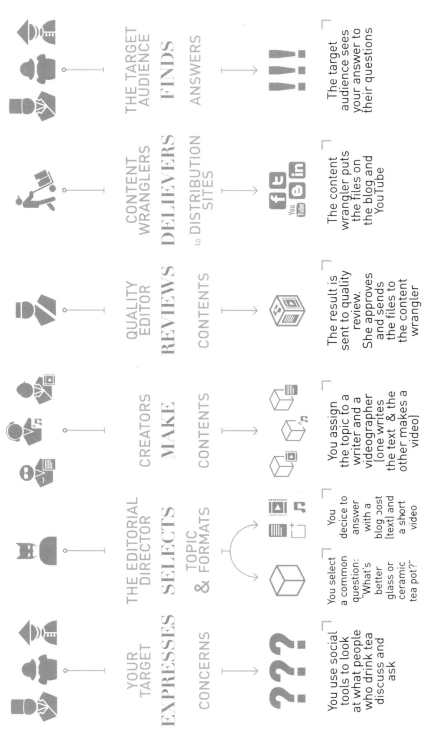

Figure 12: *An overview of the content production process as an engine.*

This is really important, so I'll repeat it: you start with your audience and you end with your audience. Figure 12 gives an graphic example of the editorial agenda. Table 2 here after also gives an overview of the process.

Step	Issue	Description	An Example
Step 1	Identify Your Audience	Know who is in your audience, such as age, sex, income, education, location, what websites they visit, and so on.	Our audience are people who drink imported green tea
Step 2	Audience's Concerns	The audience discusses many questions in social sites, feedback forms, and forums.	What's better? Keep tea in the freezer? Boil water for tea? Ceramic pots?
Step 3	Review of Topics	The editorial team collects and reviews those discussions, conversations, and questions to see what the audience is discussing.	The water temperature issue comes up frequently. We sell tea thermometers. Let's answer that one.
Step 4	Select Topics	The editorial team notices recurring topics and write these as questions.	What's the ideal temperature for hot water for green tea?
Step 5	Select the Categories and Formats	The editorial team sees if the question can be answered in various categories (text, video, images, or audio) and formats (for example, FAQs and podcasts).	Let's write an FAQ and produce a podcast on how to measure the temperature for green tea.
Step 6	Assign to Creative Staff	The editorial team assigns the questions to the creative team.	Roslyn will write the FAQ and Anastasia turns it into a voice recording for a podcast.
Step 7	Quality Control	As each item is turned in, the quality control editors reviews and approves or rejects it.	The quality editor either approves each item or rejects it with requests for changes.
Step 8	Distribution	A staffer uploads the finished items to distribution sites.	Ahsan uploads the content items to the accounts at various distribution sites.
Step 9	Reach the Audience	Your audience sees your content.	Use analytics to see traffic, leads, and sales from the content.

Table 2: *Overview of the content production as a table*

Do you see? The audience is the focus. We start with the audience. In the end, we're back to the audience. The content is built for the audience. It's customer-centric content.

4.5. Summary of this Chapter

Quite a chapter, no? We start out with an idea that everyone knows to be true, but it turns out that doesn't really work. We flip it around and put the customer at the center. Remember your customers? The reason your organization exists?

When you put your customers at the center, the search engine game is changed. Instead of doing whatever possible just to be one link at the top of a search engine, you switch to a world where you put your content wherever your customers are looking. That changes your distribution strategy.

5. Your Active Audience: 90/9/1

"Are they saying anything or are they just talking?" – Haiyan

5.1.   What's in this Chapter

Let's now look at the audience. There are different types of people in the audience who play several roles. Some of them create new ideas. Others talk about the new ideas. And the rest of the audience follows along. How does that fit into content marketing?

5.2.   The 90/9/1 Rule: Creators, Commenters, and Audience

In any social community, there are three kinds of participants:

- About 90% of the people in that community are passive participants. They read, they buy, they use.

- Some 9% of the community is commenters on that topic. They talk and write about the issues, they discuss it in public. They're also curators of content.

- 1% of the community is creators. They create the new ideas; they lead and influence the topic sufficiently to change it.

The creators set the agenda for the topic. They're the influencers. The commenters discuss whatever the creators do: they're critics, reviewers, editorialists, pundits, and so on--either as staff of a publication or self-appointed with a blog or in an online forum. The passive audience follows both the creators and the commenters.

If you can reach the 1% and get them to talk about your organization, product, or service, the commenters will pick that up and begin to discuss it. The remaining 90% will read about it. This means you can reach your audience by talking with only 1%. When influencers mention your brand, website traffic can increase by six times and conversions by two times (Eloqua). This is called *influencer marketing*.

Your content is handled in three ways, depending on the role of people in the community:

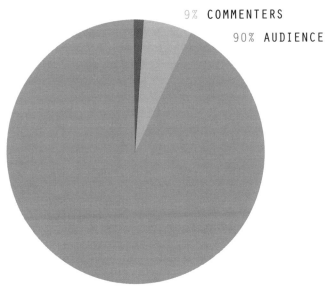

1% CREATORS

9% COMMENTERS

90% AUDIENCE

Figure 13: *The 90/9/1 Rule: Any social area is made up of consumers (90%), commenters (9%), and creators (1%). By reaching the creators, who are 1% of your audience, you reach the remaining audience.*

- Creators set the agenda and create the field. Your task is to become a creator in your field. You do this by creating authoritative content, offering leadership by advocacy, and setting an agenda.

- Commenters discuss the ideas of the 1%. Encourage the critics to comment on your content; invite bloggers and reviewers. You should do some curation to offer useful information. However, you should focus on creation, not curation.

- Consumers read and share your content. Encourage your audience to comment, rate, vote, review, modify, distribute, and share your content. You do this by offering social tools.

For example, the world of music is made up of musicians, critics, and fans. The musicians, who are in the 1%, write songs and perform music. The critics, who are in the 9%, write about the performers and the music. The fans are in the 90%, who listen to the band, buy the music, and go to concerts.

When I saw the waste in broadcast marketing at Fortune 500 companies, I began to look for more effective tools. That led me to influencer marketing. The most effective way to work with influencers is through content, which led me to content marketing.

5.3.   Is this Really 90/9/1?

I see a hand raised with a question. Someone is asking if the breakdown is precisely 90/9/1. I looked into that. Sociologists studied many kinds of groups and found the ratios depend on the group.

- Professor Akil Awan at the University of London examined jihad forums in 2005 and found 87% of the audience never posted on the forums; 13% posted at least once; 5% posted 50 times or more; and 1% posted 500 times or more.

- On Wikipedia, 50% of edits are made by 2.5% of users.

- Wildfire looked at 10,000 Facebook campaigns over nine months and found 83% of users were passive viewers, 15.4% were commenters, and 1.5% were creators.

- IBM has 433,000 employees. All employees have their own employee webpage, which includes a blog. About 6% of them (26,000) post to their blog. 1.2% (5,200) of IBM employees have posted five times or more.

In general, the ratio ranges from 0.5% to 2.5% for creators, 10% to 15% for commenters, and 85% to 90% for the passive audience.

5.4.   Your Role as a Creator: Be a Thought Leader

In any field, 1% of the participants set the field's agenda, define the topics that are discussed (and exclude the topics they don't want to discuss), and drive the future of the field. You should be a creator and be in the 1%.

- Write original research. What information is needed? What is missing? Create it and make it available. It'll spread like a California wildfire.

- Offer advocacy and leadership. Don't just participate in your field. Show that you have a clear position in your field. What should the field do? Push the field forward. See if there is necessary legislation and push it through at the state or national level.

- Present your work. Be in the public arena with your work. Speak at conferences, write articles, and publish books.

This can't be outsourced to a staffer or an outside agency. It's your career in your profession.

About 1-2% of your employees are active influencers. They're already blog-ging or tweeting. So you should support them, just as IBM supports its employees.

Find the influencers in your organization and work with them to increase their visibility. Encourage your staff to be active in social media. Give them better tools for blogging. They should blog, tweet, and so on. Collect the links to their blogs, Facebook, and Twitter accounts and post those as an official page at your site. This will give them SEO points and they will rank higher. Put them on the distribu-tion list and send them new articles. Encourage them to interview senior staff in the organization. Send them to conferences and events, both as speakers or attendees. Have your graphics team build better websites for them.

By talking positively about your organization's activities and social life, they attract clients and new employees. Outsiders see an organization with motivated employees, which increases confidence in your products and service. Their post-ings also increase your organization's digital exposure, which improves ranking in search engines and social sites.

Spouses, children, and many dogs are blogging and tweeting. They should be encouraged to mention the organization and events.

Employees should be careful in talking about strategies or upcoming prod-ucts. Gently caution your employees to avoid negative comments, such as com-plaining about low morale. Competitors can easily find and review all blogs and tweets by an organization's staff to gain insider information or measure sentiment.

However, any attempt to assert control will backfire. People will resent the control and some will write anonymous complaints.

It's impossible to prevent problems. Kids will say anything (such as KPMG Girl, whose five-minute video rant wrecked a US$23 billion company's publicity department). If the organization has built up enough good will through honesty and an open culture, it can overcome such setbacks.

The Social Employee, by Mark Burgess and Cheryl Burgess (McGraw-Hill, 2013) describes major companies actively engaged in cutting-edge social branding and social business strategies. It includes success stories from IBM, AT&T, Cisco, Dell, Adobe, and Southwest. You can learn from those examples how to apply simi-lar strategies to your own organization. The brands that leverage their employees to engage their audience through social media gain an advantage in the marketing wars.

Let's say you and I are competing in the same market. Let's assume there are 100,000 people in our market space. That means there are perhaps 1,000 influencers (1%) in that market.

Let's also assume you and I each have a $10,000 budget. I spend my budget to reach the entire market, so the effect of my marketing spend is $0.10 per person. This also means I'm spending $0.10 on each influencer in the market. If you spend your entire $10,000 on the 1,000 influencers, you're spending $10 on each influencer. Those influencers in turn will reach the entire market. The impact of our campaigns is basically ten cents versus $10. Who's going to get more impact, you or me?

This means a small but focused budget will have more impact than a large budget. You can cut your budget from $10,000 to $1,000 and you're still outspending me ten to one per influencer ($1 versus $0.10). Your $1,000 budget has more effect than my $10,000. If you focus your budget on 1% of the audience, you'll get more impact than an unfocused budget that addresses 99%.

This explains part of the power of marketing by large companies. Let's say a large company spends $3 million and a small company spends $30,000 in marketing on the same market. Both companies are marketing towards the entire market, using unfocused marketing. Let's assume the size of the market is also 100,000 people. That means the large company spends $30 per person and the small company spends $0.30 per person. The large company has more impact because they're spending $30 per person on the 1,000 people in the 1%. Both companies are wasting most of their marketing, but the large company has stronger effect.

A small company can win against a large company by carefully focusing to get more impact for their spending. The smaller company can reach the influencers. They can buy targeted mailing lists or use LinkedIn to place ads to people in the right markets and job titles.

5.7.   Tools to Find Influencers

There are a number of tools to find influencers. Here's a partial list (sorted alphabetically): Appinions, eCairn, EzyInsights, Followerwonk, Klout, Kred, Little-Bird, MentionMap, Muckrack, Nytimes.com/twitter, SocialChorus, SocialMention, Topsy, Traackr, Twazzup, and Followerwonk. New tools appear every few months.

These tools range from giving you a simple list of influencers (such as Little-Bird) to an information management platform (such as eCairn). Try these and see what works for you. If you find others, please let me know.

The least-known tool may be eCairn, yet it has the best features. It's an influencer management tool that find and ranks influencers. It also provides a set of engagement management tools. The company doesn't use broad marketing to promote itself. They use their tool to reach out to influencers who tell others about the tool, so only experts know about it.

As for finding influencers in Google+, you can use FindPeopleOnPlus.com. The tool shows a database of the 45 million people on Google+. You can enter a topic (for example, 15,300 people are interested in tea) and use filters to select by relationship, sex, age, education, workplace, occupation, country, state, and city.

Be careful with influencer tools. Some of these measure the amount of social activity on Facebook, Twitter, and so on, which is easy to fake. Thus some people are ranked highly even though they're not influencers. It also means other people are important influencers but don't rank well because their influence is mostly offline. For example, Tim Berners-Lee, who invented HTML and the Web, has only an average rank on Klout, while Justin Bieber ranks at the top of nearly every list because 20 million teenage girls can't stop talking about him. I suggest you use several tools to create lists and compare them.

The tools help you to get started by creating lists. You'll have to do the hard work of evaluating each person to create a meaningful list. Some of the companies, such as eCairn, will make lists of the influencers in your market for you.

5.8.   Measuring the Results of Influencer Marketing

We carried out a campaign for a large health insurance company. We used Klout and Twitter to find 120 people who were very active in discussion of the care for autistic children. They had a large number of followers who posted frequently; their postings were relevant to the health topic. Greg reviewed every tweet by each person for the last six months and graded them on a scale of 1 to 100 for relevancy. He reduced the list to 70 key influencers.

We wanted to measure the impact of the outreach to Twitter influencers. We took our final list of 70 Twitter people and put them in a spreadsheet with name, number of followers, our relevance score, the average number of tweets per month, and Twitter handle. We added a number ID to each one, such as T001, T002, T003, and so on, up to T070. (We used three digits in case we ever went up to several hundred and added a T to mark it as Twitter. You can use any format you like).

We then wrote out tracking tags which we could append to each URL. Each tag included that influencer's ID number.

We used Bit.ly to compress the tags, turning a long tag into a short tag with two advantages. It fit in a tweet and it hid the tracking information. We then wrote personalized emails to each influencer that included the tweet and the unique tracking tag.

This allowed us to see the results. In our web analytics program, we could see that influencer #42's tweet resulted in 14 visits but #43's resulted in 87 visits. After collecting data for a week, we sorted the list by the impact from those influencers. We ended up with a list of twelve people who could drive substantial traffic to the web page.

The purpose of the project was to increase awareness of issues for the caretakers, so there was no attempt to collect leads. However, that would have been easy to add. This project was done with nothing more than Klout, Twitter, Bit.ly, and a spreadsheet. Four people worked on this over three months.

5.9. Use Word Clouds to See What They're Saying

Some of the influencer tools include the ability to see what the influencers are saying. You select a group of influencers and use word cloud tools to see an overview of their discussion. For example, figure 14 (next page) shows the word clouds by eCairn.

5.10. Does This Work?

eCairn used influencer marketing to increase traffic to their own blog. They sent a white paper to influencers in their market space. The graph on figure 15 (next page) shows traffic to the blog:

- Before they started the influencer campaign (August 2008 to January 2009), the blog had low readership.

- In February 2009, they identified influencers, distributed a white paper, and participated in conversations.

- Readership went up to nearly 6,000 visitors in February (120 times increase).

- Afterwards, blog readership remained constant for two years at 1,000 to 2,000 readers per month (a 20 times increase over the before-period).

Interestingly, they did no further outreach after that white paper. A one-time effort increased their long-term readership by 20 times.

Figure 14: *Use eCairn to see word clouds of what influencers are discussing. Here are three groups: cloud computing, open source, and security. For example, the security group talks about malware much more than exploit kits. Screenshots were created with eCairn.*

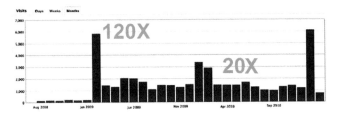

Figure 15: *Before-and-after blog traffic in an influencer outreach campaign.*

5.11. FTC Regulations on Compensation to Influencers

By the way, you should be aware of regulations on compensation or payment to influencers in the United States. The US Federal Trade Commission (FTC) requires influencers to state if they received payment, products, gifts, trips, or similar. Penalties can be US$250,000 or more per incident. To avoid penalties, influencers must state in their blog postings or tweets that they received compensation. See *FTC Guidelines on Testimonials and Endorsements*. See http://1.usa.gov/13U7Uin for more. There is similar legislation in other countries.

5.12. Your Role as a Curator and the Role of Others as Curators

Along with being a creator, you should also comment on content by other creators and offer your editorial comment on why something is useful or why it's wrong. This helps your audience see the big picture and understand the issues. It also keeps you in touch with your market.

However, your focus should be on creating new content, not curating the content of others.

Work with the commenters and curators. Offer unique content to them and help them to understand your products or services. They will promote you to their followers. You have to handle them carefully. Curators often try to insert themselves in the stream between the creators and the audience. They build a following and present themselves as important. However, they try to frame your message in their own way, so they'll change what you're saying. They may also misunderstand your message. They can have a different agenda, including promoting their favorites.

Curating shouldn't be mindless collecting. Software can copy/paste a list of 25 items. Lazy marketers create lists of "12 Secrets, 9 Tips, and 5 Basics." Anyone can spend ten minutes in a search engine, collect links, and send that out. Don't do stuff like that. Curation is an active process where you select useful items and add your comments. When you tell people why something is important, you guide others.

You can also curate your own content. Make a list of the whitepapers, research, slideware, videos, webcasts, and so on, which you produced last quarter. Add short summaries and why they're useful. Post this monthly or quarterly to your blog and distribute it.

Curation isn't just for small sites. Yahoo! started as a curation site. Jerry Yang collected links to websites. Yahoo! News, Google News, TechCrunch, and others are curators.

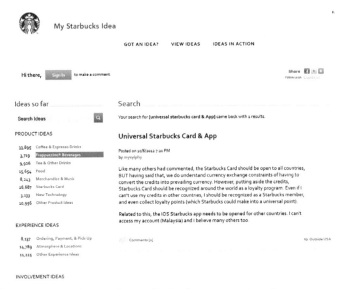

Figure 16: *MyStarbucksIdea.com invites Starbucks customers to make suggestions and discuss.*

It's easy to automate the collection and distribution of content. Here are several curation tools (alphabetical): Alltop, Curata, CurationSoft, CurationStation, DayLife, Equentia, Flipboard, Google News, Lingospot, Loud3r, OneSpot, Perfect-Market, PopURLS, PublishThis, Scoop.It, SmartBrief, Storify, Techcrunch, Techmeme, and Yahoo! News.

5.13. Your Audience: The 90%

90% of a community is generally passive. Up to the 1990s, people who watched TV had little, if any, ability to engage with the creators or commentators. Web 2.0 changed this by putting a range of tools in the audience's hands that allow them to talk and share with each other. You should add Web 2.0 social tools wherever possible on your website and products. Encourage your audience to comment, rate, vote, review, share, distribute, modify, and distribute your content.

Some companies have built websites as a community site or suggestion box for their audience. The best-known example is MyStarbucksIdea.com, where people can suggest ideas for Starbucks and vote on ideas by others.

Many companies shudder at the idea of losing control. But they've already lost control. Just about every social media strategist has met clients who state that they don't use Facebook or Twitter because they don't want the conversation to get out of control. Just like the other social media strategists, I open Facebook and Twitter, search for the company name and products, and show them what is being said. The conversation is already there; they just don't know it, and because they're not involved, they have no influence.

People may be talking about an organization without the organization's knowledge, but there's something worse: nobody talking about it. If there is no conversation about your organization, products, or services, you have no presence in the market. Your audience doesn't know you exist. That's easy to fix.

5.14. Your Active Audience and User Generated Content (UGC)

User-generated content (UGC) is a fancy way to say that your audience is creating content about you.

The first step is to give them comment boxes so they can talk about your organization. Make it easy for them to discuss and rate your content, products, and services.

Go beyond that. Encourage them to modify your content and products. Release the files for videos and images so people can modify these and let them upload the changes to your website. Barnes & Noble realized that computer people were buying Nook tablets and installing Ubuntu Linux (an operating system). Barnes & Noble offered them internal developer information that increased sales of the Nook.

This is called *product hacking*, which has created a lively community of people who change things and pass around the ideas. Encourage your audience to modify your products and get them to tell you about it. Hold contests for clever ideas, write about their work in your blog, and show off their results. For example, see IkeaHackers.net, a site by Jules Yap, where people come up with clever ideas to change Ikea products. (Ikea had nothing to do with that site). There's also Makezine.com and Instructables.com. Some guy named Steve Wozniak was doing product hacking which led him to start a small company that changed everything.

See how your customers are modifying your products and offer kits and information to help them.

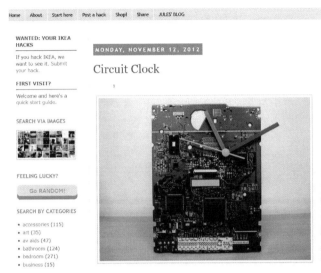

Figure 17: *MyStarbucksIdea.com invites Starbucks customers to make suggestions and discuss.*

5.15. Summary of this Chapter

The audience isn't just listening to you. Some of them are actively creating new ideas. You should know who they are and be in touch with them. By reaching the 1% influencers, they talk about you and you'll reach the 99%

The critics love to discuss, review, and comment on whatever is happening in their field. Engage with them, offer them information, and work with them.

90% of your audience is active listeners, which means they follow the influencers, see what the critics say, and then share and discuss with their friends and colleagues. They want to help each other, so they will share useful information.

CASE STUDY: SONY XPERIA

To keep an audience's interest in the brand, the organization must take care to consider what the audience thinks of the company. When Sony launched their Xperia smart phone in Australia in 2011, they suffered an image problem after because customers used the Sony Facebook page to express their frustration with the service. In response, Sony carried out "The Xperia Social Xperiment." They locked Tommy Little, an Australian comedian, in a room for eight hours with an Xperia phone. Sony's Facebook page encouraged fans invited to call him and tell him to do whatever they wanted. The event was broadcast via the Facebook page. Fans were rewarded with prizes. The goal was to encourage fans to express freely on the brand page and have fun at the same time.

NEGATIVE BRAND PERCEPTION

XPERIA XPERIMENTS

POSITIVE BRAND PERCEPTION

January 2012: negative posts multiply on the official Sony Facebook page.

A one day marathon experience allow Facebook fans of Sony to ask famous comedian ERTYUIRT to do anything they want, using solely his Sony Xperia smartphone.

February 2012: a few days after the event, positive comments are back. The halo effect goes beyond the awareness on the event.

6. SEO and Content Marketing: Be Findable

6.1.   What's in this Chapter

So you produce your content and put it on the web. How are people going to find it? You have to make sure people can find your content. When it was a matter of getting a web page to show up in a search engine, we called it SEO (*Search Engine Optimization*, or adjusting the page so it could be indexed by a search engine). But search engines are now just one piece of the game. Instead of text, you're creating images, video, and sound. Instead of web pages, you're placing content on social media sites and so on. And people are using tablets and smart phones now.

So the real question is:

"How do I make sure people can find my content, wherever they're looking?"

That's what I call this *findability*.

6.2.   Offer Answers to Your Audience's Questions

Search engines tell you to write good content. That's easy now because you can use Web 2.0 tools to find out what people want. Look at the comments on your site, the questions in Yahoo! Answers and Quora, the questions to your support team, the rankings and ratings, and so on. Write replies, FAQs, support pages, ebooks, and so on. Look at your audience's interests and write for them.

As for your audience, they have to be able to find your content. Quite simply, if they can't see it, your organization doesn't exist.

The best way to make sure your audience sees your content is to create very good content. This makes distribution very easy: just release it. If you create meaningful or useful content, people will find it and share it with others. People will add links to it from their web pages, blogs, Facebook pages, and so on. They'll tweet about it. They'll copy your PDFs and infographics and pass them around to others.

STARTED RESEARCH WITH USA

TRAVEL RELATED WEBSITES — 125
SEARCH ENGINES — 71
PRODUCT/PRICE COMPARISON WEBSITES — 31
WORD OF MOUTH — 24
ADVERTISING
VIDEO PORTALS
BLOGS/FORUMS OR CONSUMER REVIEWS
ONLINE ARTICLES
TV PROGRAM
RADIO PROGRAM
BROCHURES OR CATALOGUES
NEWSPAPER ARTICLES
BOOKS

Figure 18: *The ConsumerBarometer graph shows where people in the United States research travel information. For clarity, I measured the bars and added numbers.*

6.3. Where Do People Research?

Remember the buying funnel? People start by researching. So where do they research?

One way to find out is with ConsumerBarometer.com, a project by Google, IAB Europe (the Interactive Advertising Bureau), and TNS (a consultant group). They used polls and consumer data to show how people research in the process of purchasing. It covers 38 countries in 35 product categories, including automotive, finance, real estate, retail, technology, and travel. They interviewed 2,500 people in each country.

For example, how do business travelers search for business travel? If they're in the awareness and consideration phase of the buying funnel, where do they look?

This shows that of the 2,500 US interviewees, 125 people researched business travel by using travel-related websites and 71 people used search engines. If you consider that Google has a 66.7% share of the US search market (Comscore, January 2013), then 47 people used Google for research. This means 2.7 times as many chose travel sites over Google.

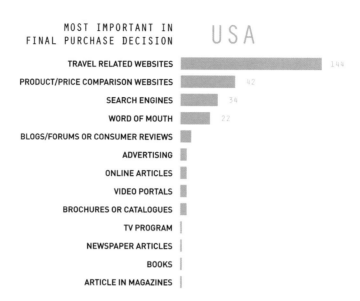

MOST IMPORTANT IN
FINAL PURCHASE DECISION   U S A

TRAVEL RELATED WEBSITES	144
PRODUCT/PRICE COMPARISON WEBSITES	42
SEARCH ENGINES	34
WORD OF MOUTH	22
BLOGS/FORUMS OR CONSUMER REVIEWS	
ADVERTISING	
ONLINE ARTICLES	
VIDEO PORTALS	
BROCHURES OR CATALOGUES	
TV PROGRAM	
NEWSPAPER ARTICLES	
BOOKS	
ARTICLE IN MAGAZINES	

Figure 19: *This graph from ConsumerBarometer shows which resources people in the United States considered in the final decision for travel.*

A company that wants to attract business travelers (such as hotels for business travel, airlines, and car rental services) should put more effort at showing up on those travel sites than search engines. They shouldn't ignore the search engines, but those shouldn't be their primary placement.

What about the purchase decision? Which websites affect their decision in the purchase phase?

Again, for clarity, I measured the bars and added numbers.

For the 2,500 US interviewees, 144 people based their decision on travel-related websites and 42 used comparison sites for their decision. For 34 people, search engines were the important factor in the decision (of those 34 people, 23 used Google, or nearly the same as word-of-mouth). This means 8 times as many people used travel-related sites and price comparison websites over Google.

This kind of information doesn't show up in your web analytics report. Web analytics only shows information about the people who come to your site. It doesn't show what people are doing at other sites.

What do we learn by looking at Consumer Barometer? You must improve your findability in other websites, not just search engines. If a business hotel in Chicago wants to attract business travelers, they should place articles about their hotel on business travel sites, such as review sites of business hotels and blogs for business travelers.

Try Consumer Barometer to see if you can find how your audience searches for your services and products.

6.4.   Spamming Google Isn't Easy Anymore

Technical SEO was what we called the collection of methods to optimize a page for search engines. These were the changes that were made to a web page, including meta-tags, keywords, links, site structure, and file names. That worked pretty well for a while, but it doesn't have much effect anymore. Here's some information:

- You want to optimize for Google's search algorithm. Okay... which Google algorithm? Google is constantly testing their algorithm, so they run several versions of the algorithm at the same time and compare the results. According to Google, there can be 50 to 200 active versions of the algorithm. Nobody can "optimize for the algorithm" because even if they had a copy of the algorithm, there are other versions.

- Search results depend on your location. People in Nashville and Berlin will get different results for the same search. So if someone promises to make you #1 in Google, you may be number one in your city, but nowhere else.

- Google has a team of 10,000 people who evaluate the quality of a webpage's content. They use a list of criteria to increase the ranking of good pages and lower the ranking of poor content. They also flag pages as spam. None of the methods of technical SEO matter to their evaluation. I know this because I have a collection of Quality Rater manuals and I've used the Quality Rater tool to evaluate sites. Bing and Yahoo! have similar teams.

Google's ranking method also looks at social activity, including the number of Google+ votes, clicks from Google to the site, volume of traffic, and similar. A page may use all of the tricks of technical SEO, but if it has a low amount of social activity, the page won't show up.

The search results also differ by platform. This also makes sense, since you'll have different intentions whether you're searching from your desktop computer or cell phone. Try it. Search for "pizza" on your cell phone and your desktop computer and compare the results (see Figure 20).

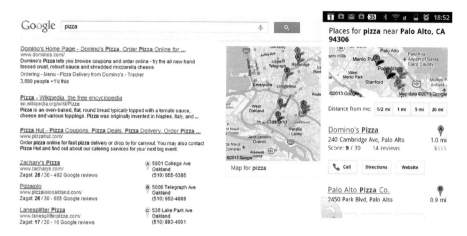

Figure 20: *Comparison of search results in desktop computers and phones. The phone result shows only restaurant names, street address, and "Call Now" buttons.*

Why the difference? Michelle at work is probably thinking about pizza for tonight so a search on her desktop computer shows information that allows her to evaluate pizza restaurants. But when she's using a cell phone, she's looking for pizza nearby. All she needs is an address and a call-now button.

Both searches were made at the same time. The search on my phone included my location (Palo Alto) but the search on my computer placed me 50 miles away in Oakland.

6.5. Hacking the Google Algorithm

Nevertheless, many organizations want quick results and they're willing to cut to the front of the line.

Go to any search engine and search for "black hat SEO." You can hire your own Russian hacker at BlackHatWorld.com who will make you #1 for only $25.

Whoa, partner! You may show up for a day or two in a search engine, but they automatically notice pages that jump up in ranking. The search engine sends your page to their quality raters who review your page, note its poor quality, and down-rank it. Once your page has been flagged as low quality, you will on page 23 forever. Гаснут свечи, кончен бал. That's Russian for "Game Over!"

6.6.   But I Need Sales or I'll Get Fired!

Even though I tell people the truth about SEO, they still want the magic bean that will bring millions of visitors to their website.

Are there legitimate SEO companies? Well, what counts as SEO? You can use technical methods to show up at the top of search engines but your page will be reviewed by humans who will compare your page against the other pages for that result. It's not the technical methods, keywords, links, or tricks. It's the quality of the information that counts.

SEO makes your page technically compliant with search engines. This gets your page into the search engine's index, but that's all it does. Whether your page will be on page one is up to the quality of your page.

So now you're beginning to realize the big secret about "the search algorithm." There isn't one. Search engines have tools for indexing and managing the database of a hundred billion URLs, but they use people to evaluate and select the ten results for page one. This works pretty well for the top search queries, which make up 99.99% of searches and that's good enough. For less common queries, search engines use software, which is why the first few results are okay, but they quickly become random. That means those links weren't reviewed by humans.

6.7.   Why You Shouldn't Rely on SEO

Companies often tell me "We're #1 in the search engine for our main keyword. We don't need to pay for marketing."

That's really good. They're getting lots of traffic for free.

But what is going to happen when the search engine changes the ranking and the company drops to page 24? Traffic and sales will collapse 90% in one day. Within a week, the company will have to lay off most of their employees. Without a sales team, how will they build up again?

Why does this happen? Search engines change their rules. Why? Who knows? But they do this frequently. Anyone who works in SEO can tell you stories about desperate phone calls begging "You gotta get us back in the search engines!"

The search engines change the rules and they won't answer calls. No explanations, no help.

So you get the picture. If you rely on search engines for most of your traffic and sales, that could disappear one day. There will be very little you can do. Don't put your eggs in one basket.

I've noticed in the last few years there has been a general decline in traffic to a number of large sites from search engines. It's not clear why. It's possible that people are moving over to mobile devices (tablets and phones), they're using apps, or they blocking cookies. Look at your web analytics for the last ten years. Look at Google Trends, which shows keyword trends from 2004 to today, and see if there is a trend. Compare your traffic with your competitors, top keywords for your market, and so on.

6.8.   What about SEO Hackers?

There are hundreds of companies that call you and promise to make you number one in the search engines. They identify phrases for you and add links to make you number one for that phrase. How does this work?

It's easy to be number one for an obscure phrase. Find a phrase with little competition, put a handful of links on fake sites, and you're number one. But nobody searches for those phrases. The SEO companies that offer this are just scams.

6.9.   So How Do You Get on Page One?

It's a question of who is looking: you or your audience.

Most SEO is done for the sake of the company. This means the company wants to see itself at the top of the search engines in a search for a keyword that the company thinks is important. The SEO expert therefore puts her efforts in getting that keyword to the top of the search engine.

But it's not the company that is searching, it's the audience. Most SEO is actually "vanity SEO"; the company wants to see itself whenever it looks in the mirror.

So the real question is how to show up when the audience searches. Which brings up the question, how are they searching?

Your audience is searching for solutions to their problems. They're typing queries such as:
- What's the best business hotel in Chicago?
- What are the top ten things to do in Paris?
- How do I make pancake mix without eggs?

Look at your customers' emails to your support desk. Look at the queries in your website's search box. Look at Yahoo! Answers, Quora, and so on. Copy the last six months of tweets. Print out all of these, hold a team meeting, and go through these, one by one. This is what your audience wants to know. Answer these. Write articles and make videos. Those replies will show up in the search engines. People will copy your information and email it to their friends, post it to their blogs and Twitters, and so on. Good information distributes itself.

Let's say you want to start a small business to sell Aunt Azizeh's pancake mix, just like the pancakes she made back in Iran. Everyone loves the pancakes and you think it could be a business.

You search Twitter, Facebook, and Yahoo! Answers and you see a common thread "How do I make a pancake mix where I just add water?"

So you use your cell phone to make a video and you write an FAQ where you post the recipe and add "Make this really easy: order two pounds of Aunt Azizeh's Homemade Pancake Mix. Free shipping." Many people aren't going to take the time to look for egg powder or the right kind of whole wheat flour. When they see how easy it is to use the mix and how delicious it looks, they'll just buy from you.

Your video will be on the first page, because the search engines' quality reviewers are looking for a good video on that topic and they'll pick yours. The quality raters aren't experts. The search engines don't hire technical experts for this. They want average people with a general background who see the web pretty much in the same way as the general audience. So you don't have to create a page for review by an MIT professor. If your uncle in Ohio is impressed, that'll be good enough for the quality raters.

But don't put all of your money on the search engine. Place your content in all other channels. The more pages that talk about you, the more likely your audience will see you. Luckily for you, most of those sites don't have an army of people who reject pages. So your chances of placement are better outside of the search engines.

6.10. The Best SEO Tools

Some of the best SEO tools are free:

- **Marketing.Grader.com:** First, find what's broken or weak at your website. Use Hubspot's Marketing Grader to get a report on the state of your website. Print it and give it to your webmaster to fix. Free.

- **Bing Webmaster Tools:** This shows you the number of links to each page, top keywords, and traffic. It'll find broken links. You can submit XML sitemaps. It also notifies you of errors that prevent indexing. Free.

- **Google Webmaster Tools:** This also shows you the top keywords that bring traffic to your site, the ranking in Google for keywords and pages, and more. You can submit XML sitemaps. It also notifies you of errors that prevent indexing. It'll find broken links. Free.

- **Microsoft Search Engine Optimization Toolkit:** Helps you to identify problems and fix them. Free.

I strongly recommend that you use both of the Webmaster Tools from Bing and Google. In the United States, Google has 67% and Bing plus Yahoo! has 28% share of the market. Together, they have 95%, so by using both, you're covered in search engines. China uses Baidu and Russia uses Yandex as search engines. If your market includes China or Russia, make sure your content can be indexed by their search engines. Table 3 gives a global insight on the search engine market:

Search Engine	Reach	Searches	Share
Google	Global	114.73	65.2%
Baidu	China	14.50	8.2%
Yahoo!	Global	8.63	4.9%
Yandex	Russia	4.84	2.8%
Bing	Global	4.48	2.5%
Other	Other	28.79	16.4%
Total		175.97	100%

Table 3: *2012 comScore qSearch: Overview Global search engine market*

Searches = The number of searches in billions in 60 days (November and December, 2012). For example, there were 4.48 billion searches in Bing in November and December, 2012.

Remember that Yahoo!'s search engine is powered by Bing, so Bing's total share includes both Yahoo! and Bing.

"Other" is made up of hundreds of small search engines, such as Blekko, Dogpile, and DuckDuckGo. Combined, they have twice as many searches as Baidu, and almost as many as Baidu, Yahoo!, Yandex, and Bing combined. Make sure your content is search-engine compliant so the baby search engines can pick it up.

There are a number of keyword tools from SEO companies. They promise that you'll get long-tail keywords that bring traffic. Let's look at keywords.

6.11. The Mystery of Keywords

There seems to be a mystery around keywords. Some people think if they only had the right keyword, their page would be number one. You know by now it doesn't work that way.

Still, there's a bit to that. Your audience uses keywords to searching for topics, so if you use those keywords, you have a better chance to show up.

I didn't say you will show up for sure. There are examples of pages without any keywords whatsoever that show up as number one, such as images that match precisely what people are searching. (How does that happen? The quality raters looked for the best image that matches the query).

Keword discovery is easy (I'm giving away all the SEO secrets today):

- Use your web analytics tool, such a Webtrends, Google Analytics, Coremetrics, or Omniture. These show you that people use to find your site in search engines.

- You can also try Keyword.Discovery.com, WordTracker.com, and Wordstream. com.

- Test keywords with a short campaign in Google AdWords. It'll quickly show you if there is traffic for that keyword.

Find perhaps two or three high-traffic keywords for your page and use those at the beginning of the TITLE tag, DESCRIPTION tag, the heading, and in the links. Why at the beginning? Eye-tracking studies show that people scan the first four or five words of a heading or paragraph. If it has what they're looking for, they will read more. If not, they leave. So this isn't for the search engine's sake. It's for your readers.

This isn't a technical trick to get the search engine to rank the page higher. By using these words, your audience will quickly know the page may be what they're looking for and they may read further. But if the page has low quality content, magic keywords are useless.

Let's cover the steps to ensure compliance with search engines. Here's what you need to do:

- **TITLE meta-tag:** Put your top keywords at the front. Use up to 66 characters, including spaces.

- **DESCRIPTION meta-tag:** Put your top keywords at the front. Use up to 155 characters, including spaces.

- **Heading:** The page should have a heading that uses an H1 HTML heading format. The heading should be an informative summary of the page. Put your top keywords in the first three words.

- **Body text:** You're writing for your audience, not computers. Write text that is useful and informative. Adding lots of keywords won't help and may actually lead the quality raters to lower the page's ranking.

- **Active links from other pages:** At any page from your website that is already in the search engine, add a link to the new page. Make sure the link works. The search engines will find the link, follow it to your new page, and add the page to its index. You don't need to pay to submit pages. If you want to submit pages, use Webmaster Tools, which are free.

- **XML sitemap:** This is optional. For a while, Flash and JavaScript prevented search engines from following links. So XML sitemaps were invented as a solution. An XML sitemap: is a list of pages at your site. You submit this list to the search engines (use the webmaster tools). I do it to ensure all pages are indexed, but as I said, if there's a link to your page, it'll be indexed.

What about SEO companies with engineers who use software to do SEO for 500,000 pages? They're using software because there are so many pages, but they're basically doing the same thing. They standardize the pages so their software can insert the top keywords into the TITLE, DESCRIPTION, heading, and so on. Does that give them an advantage in ranking? No. That makes the pages search engine compliant, which means they can be indexed. That's all.

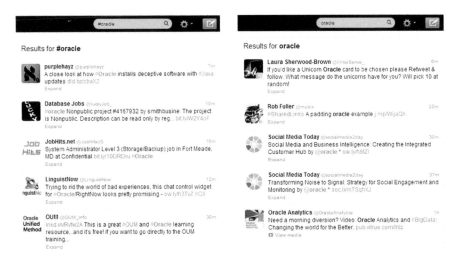

Figure 21: *Here are the results for a search in Twitter for #oracle vs. oracle..*

6.13. SEO for Social: Search Boxes on Social Media Sites

The various social sites have their own search engines. These range from somewhat okay to simple. They can generally find search terms, but they lack relevance, authority scores, and other ways to rank the results. They also don't have humans to evaluate the results. There are no meta-tags for pages in Facebook or Twitter.

The search engines at social media sites are intentionally simple. Let's say you and I are aeronautics engineers. If you have a useful astronomy app for your cell phone, you'll talk about it and since I'm connected to you in Facebook, I'll read your postings about it and I'll start using it. You and I share the same interests, so we'll share knowledge. My brother, who is a lawyer, isn't interested in astronomy so the app won't be relevant to him. Facebook feels information will be shared naturally within social groups which means members don't really need to search. In fact, if you're searching for something, maybe you don't really need it. That's why a search engine goes against the point of a social media site. Social media sites put emphasis on the use of social relationships to spread information, not search.

This applies to content marketing. If you create very useful content, it'll be distributed by your audience. They want to help their friends, so they'll share your content. The best way to distribute your content through social media is to get the influencers in your audience to talk about your content, organization, or products.

6.14. Twitter and Hashtags

Twitter's search box is very simple in comparison to Bing or Google. The results are ranked only by date (newest first). Tweets aren't reviewed by humans.

- Because there are only 140 characters and no meta-information, Twitter searches the body of the tweet. If the word appears in a tweet, Twitter will find it. But Twitter won't find plurals or related terms.

- However, nobody scrolls beyond a few pages. If your tweet was written two months ago, nobody will see it.

There's quite a bit of confusion around hashtags. A hashtag is a keyword with a hash mark ("#"), such as #oracle. Hashtags are also written as one word, such as #IBMBrazil. Twitter search doesn't care if it's upper case or lower case. That's all there is to hashtags.

You should develop a hashtag for your organization, product, or service. Search to see if anyone else is using it. Type it in lower case to make sure it doesn't have an inadvertent meaning. Use it in your marketing and documents. Use it when you post to Twitter. People will begin to follow it.

Twitter's search shows different results for a word with or without a hashtag. Figure 21 are the results for searches for "#oracle" and "oracle". You can't register, reserve, buy, or copyright a hashtag. Anyone can use it. If a company spends money to develop a hashtag, someone else can use it to get attention in that company's audience. For example, IBM Brazil holds a conference and uses the hashtag #IBMBrazil. Others can use the same hashtag and their tweets will show up to conference attendees who are following the tag

6.15. Your Website's Navigation to Your Content

When you create content, be sure your website is easy to navigate.

- People should be able to land at any page in your website and quickly get to the pages with FAQs, case studies, and so on.

- They should be able to use the search box to find your content.

- The links should allow search engines to scan your pages to index your content.

If you have great content but lousy navigation, your content is hidden. The best rule is to keep it simple.

6.16. Can You Post the Same Content on Different Pages?

That question has two sides. If you post an article to your blog and the same material to other pages, whether on your site or other sites, the search engines will ignore those extra copies. It uses the earliest version of the file. There isn't a penalty for duplicate content. The extra copies just won't show up.

However, that doesn't matter for you. As you've seen, many people use sites other than Google to look for something. If copies of your article show up on other sites, your audience will see those.

6.17. Link Building and Inbound Links for Content Marketing

The more links you have, the more likely people will stumble across those links and come to your page. This means you should build up a presence in other web pages.

The Webmaster Tools at both Bing and Google will tell you the number of links from other pages to your site. You can also use ahrefs.com, MajesticSEO.com and OpenSiteExplorer.org to see how many incoming links you have.

You can wait for people to find your page and add links on their own. This used to be pretty common during Web 1.0 when we all felt that we were building the web together.

But the commercialization of the web led people to be reluctant to create links for free for companies. This means you have to ask people to link to your site.

We managed large-scale link building projects for many companies. This can have a 30% success rate (which means about a third of sites will add the link). (Don't ask me to do this; I'm just telling you so you'll know how it works).

Your success rate depends on the quality of your page. People won't link to low-quality sites. If you produce good content (meaningful, useful, authoritative), people are likely to link to it from their web pages, blogs, Facebook pages, and so on. They'll tweet about your content. If you distribute PDFs, Powerpoints, infographics, and so on, they'll copy these and post them on their web pages and blogs.

6.18. SEO for Photos: Yes, You Can!

Since I've written about images in content marketing, you may wonder how search engines handle images. How do you do SEO if there are no keywords?

It turns out Google is pretty good at image recognition. Add the Google Goggles app to your smart phone and scan various things, such as book covers, wine bottles, and stuff in your refrigerator. It can identify them. On your desktop computer, search for art work, such as paintings by Sanford Robinson Gifford (1823-1880). Pick one at random and point your phone at it. Google Goggles will tell you the artist's name and title of the painting. Point Goggles at landmarks, such as bridges, cathedrals, and buildings (you can also use photos from your travels). It can also identify most cars.

You can also search images on your desktop computer at images.google.com. Take a photo of something and see if Google can identify it.

How do you do SEO for images? Help the search engines by adding a clear large photo of your logo, products, and packaging. Add your keywords to the page. Use your keyword in the file name.

6.19. Summary of this Chapter

You're wondering what you should do for SEO. You now know your audience is more likely to go to expert pages instead of searching at Google.

- Create good content. Find out what people want and answer those questions. People will link to your articles, photos, and videos. People will link to these items and share them with their friends. The reviewers at search engines will select these articles for the top results.

- Your audience looks at more than search engines. Send your content (or links to your content) to the influencers and top sites for your audience. Place your content in as many relevant locations as possible.

- Make sure your content is "search engine compliant," which means it has meta-tags, keywords, and links so search engines can find it and index it. Use SEO, but focus on creating good content.

If I have to say it in one sentence, your best solution is to find out what your audience wants and write the very best article for them. You won't have to use marketing or advertising. Just release it to a few people. They will find it so useful that they'll share it with their friends. Your article, video, or podcast will appear in thousands of websites and blogs. People will tweet about it. It will spread on its own.

How do you write such an article? Understand what the audience wants. Research your field and become the leading expert in it. Hire very good writers.

7. Advertising's Role in Content Marketing

7.1. What's in this Chapter

So you've written great content. You can wait for people to discover it on their own. Or you can speed it up with advertising to let people know what you have. A strong ad campaign can reach your audience within days. If you know your cost-per-lead (CPL) and cost-per-action (CPA), advertising is profitable.

7.2. What Is Digital Advertising?

First of all, this field has several names. These include paid search, paid placement, banner placement, and pay-per-click (PPC). The billing method can include CPM and PPC. I prefer to call it PPC because it's clear: You pay for the click.

PPC started out as the placement of small text ads in search engines, beginning with GoTo.com and Yahoo! In 2002, Google added PPC to their search engine.

For the first time, you could track displays, clicks, and conversions down to the penny. You knew precisely how much each click cost and how much you had spent to get a conversion.

PPC lets you place your ad at the top of the search engines. You can launch nationwide (or global) campaigns literally in minutes.

Because PPC shows you the number of ad displays and clicks on your ads, you can test to find the headings for e-mails and slogans for ad campaigns that produce the best response. You can test a list of keywords and find which ones get the most traffic. You can use A/B split testing and quickly find the optimal selling price for your products.

7.3.   How to Pay: CPM or PPC

There are two ways to pay for digital ads: CPM and PPC.

- **Cost-per-Mille (CPM):** CPM is the price to display 1,000 ads. For example, ads may be $3 CPM, which means you'll pay $3 for 1,000 ads to be shown to your audience. You pay for the display of the ads, not the clicks. If you want to show 100,000 ads, you buy 100 blocks of CPMs at $3 each. ("Mille" is 1,000 in Latin).

- **Pay-per-Click (PPC):** As the name says, you pay for each click. The ad can be shown 100,000 times, but if five people click the ad, you pay for only five clicks. You pay for the click, not the display.

7.4.   Does PPC Work?

Some people will say PPC doesn't work.

A PPC campaign can be managed to meet CPL or CPA targets. If you know the maximum cost-per-lead is $72.15, you can manage the bids to stay under that number.

As long as advertising delivers results within your CPL or CPA, the PPC will work. You should use it. Well-managed advertising can be quite effective and profitable.

I know it works: I've set up and managed over 250 PPC campaigns since 2002 for a wide range of clients in markets such as online storage, financial services, banking, real estate, online video, hotel, travel, business schools, shoes, lawyers, cars, universities, online games, magazines, business consulting, call centers, resorts, carpet cleaning, semiconductor testing tools, cosmetics, fitness, cemeteries, and restaurants.

I've often worked with clients who didn't know their CPLs. I discovered they were paying four or six times the maximum CPL, which meant they were losing money. Within weeks, I brought the CPLs and CPAs down to the target value. I did that by using A/B split testing of ads, multivariate testing of landing pages, and by managing bids to the target CPL or CPA.

Why do some people say it doesn't work? It didn't work for them because they didn't understand it. There are subtle technical issues to PPC management. The failure to manage accounts with CPL or CPA is also widespread. Many of my clients didn't know how to calculate their CPLs. I also often see competitors over-bid, which means they're losing money. The search engines won't help you because they don't know how to calculate your CPLs.

You can learn how to calculate your CPL and CPA. Get my free ebook at the book's Resources page.

7.5.   How to Set Up and Manage PPC

This is a book on content marketing, not PPC, so I won't give you a manual on how to set up or manage PPC in Google AdWords, Bing, and so on. There are plenty of resources for that. Here are the two best ones:

- Advanced Google AdWords, by Brad Geddes (Sybex, 2nd ed., 2012, US$39.99). This is an excellent guide to PPC by the leading expert. Brad knows Google AdWords better than Google. I've known Brad for a long time and he's really dedicated to this. I have pretty much all of the books on PPC and his is the best. Get this book for the person who manages your PPC account.

- *Search Engine Marketing,* by me (McGraw-Hill, 2010). My book has a chapter on PPC. In a quick overview in 62 pages, you'll understand what's going on so you can direct your team. See the book's Resources page.

7.6.   What to Avoid in PPC

Instead of what to do in PPC, I have listed a few things that shouldn't be done (See Table 4 next page).

You'll notice there are quite a few penalties in that list. Google forces advertisers to be more efficient. Google punishes poor-performing or inactive accounts by lowering the ranking and increasing the cost-per-click. Google rewards well-managed accounts by increasing the ranking and lowering the cost-per-click. I've managed many accounts where I bid $2 yet pay only $0.15 and be #1.

Incidentally, the table also tells you what your budget should be. Google wants to see 100 clicks per day for a US nationwide campaign. Set up your account, improve it, and look at the average cost-per-click (CPC). If it's $2, then you'll have to pay $200 per day ($6,000 per month). If you pay less than that, Google will lower your ranking and increase your CPC. (The number of clicks depends on the country).

Mistake	Explanation	Solution
Text ads and image ads in the same ad group	Google uses different algorithms for text and image ads. If they're in the same ad group, image ads will perform poorly.	Put text ads and image ads in different ad groups.
Flat bids	The same bid for every keyword. A sign of a zombie account is the same bid for every keyword. The account was set up poorly and then left alone.	Manage the bid for each keyword.
Click-through-rate (CTR) under 1%.	The average click-through rate (CTR) for an ad group should be 1% or greater. Google penalizes poor ad groups by lowering their position and increasing the cost per click (CPC).	Pause keywords that have CTRs under 1%.
Under 100 clicks per day	If the account has fewer than 100 clicks per day for a US nationwide account, Google will penalize it by lowering the ad position and increasing the cost-per-click.	Increase the budget to get 100 clicks per day. Use better keywords and ads to get more clicks.
Many key words in an ad group	If there are too many keywords, Google computer won't be able to identify the main keyword of the ad group.	Use at most five key words per ad group.
Lack of negative key words	Use negative key words so your ads won't show up for non-relevant searches.	Use negative keywords.
Inactive management of the account	Another clue to a poorly-managed account is low activity. Google looks to see how often you log into the account to make changes. If there is low activity, Google will lower the ad positions and increase the cost-per-click.	Manage the account at least weekly.
No conversion tracking.	You need conversion tracking to know if the account makes money or not.	Set up conversion tracking.
No web analytics	You need analytics to know if traffic goes up or down. It provides many other useful reports.	Set up web analytics.

Table 4: PPC - Nine mistakes to avoid.

Figure 22: *The ads on the right are text ads. The ad on the left is a banner ad. Ads come in eight shapes, such as tall, wide, or rectangular.*

Any competent PPC person can manage your accounts. Get my ebook and Brad Geddes' book and assign this to your PPC manager. How to tell if someone is competent? Ask him questions from the list. How do you calculate the CPL? How do you manage bids to reach that CPL? How many clicks per day should an account have? How often do you manage bids? See what he says.

The good news is most of your competitors don't know what they're doing. Over 90% of people who use PPC set up basic accounts, enter their credit card information, and walk away. Several million zombie accounts send a few hundred dollars every month to the search engines. Do these accounts produce sales or profits? Nobody knows. I'm not just talking about little accounts. I looked at a Very Large Company's account that was spending over US$1 million per month. Every few weeks, someone changed a few keywords. At another Really Large Company (all of you have used their services), I saw they paid US$1,200 to sell a US$300 item.

7.7. Text Ads or Banner Ads?

There are two kinds of PPC ads: text and banner. Text ads have a heading, two short lines of text, and a URL. Banner ads however use images and text. Figure 22 give an example of this.

Banner ads are more effective because they allow you to show different kinds of messages in the same ad. You can show a photo of the person or product, offer something ("Contest: See Her Live!"), add another offer (listen to her song), and include a call-to-action for additional content ("Slide Show: Images of Natalie.")

Figure 23: *An example of a banner ad from Salesforce.com that includes their logo, font, and colors.*

Use trained graphics people to make your banner ads. I've tested this and found better design gets higher response.

Try both text and banner ads and see which works best.

The campaign setup for banner ads isn't the same as for text ads. Banner ads use a different technology. If you mix banner ads and text ads in the same ad group, the results will be poor. Look into this and learn how to manage this.

7.8.   Use Branding in Your Banner Ads

Use your branding guidelines to design your banner ads. This includes your logo, fonts, and colors. The ad should reinforce the overall look of your organization to strengthen recognition and recall.

In figure 23, for example, Salesforce use their company colors and logo in their ad.

7.9.   Use Banner Ads and Influencers to Reach Your Audience

Here is how to use banner ads in influencer marketing:

- Identify the top topics that your influencers are discussing. This shows you the topics that are important to them.

- Create banner ads that include those words.

Figure 24: *Here's an example of a HootSuite ad at my site. HootSuite targeted my website and placed their ad on my page because I talk about Twitter on that page.*

- Place your ads in their blogs. With eCairn, you can see which bloggers are using the various ad distribution platforms (such as Google AdWords, Yahoo!, Microsoft Advertising, Federated Media and so on). For example, there are 317 bloggers who are influencers for digital advertising. Forty-five of them use Google AdWords; five use DoubleClick, and three use Federated Media. You then place ads in Google AdWords, DoubleClick, and Federated Media.

- Make a list of blog URLs and use URL targeting in PPC to place ads on those URLs (and only those sites). Your ads appear on the bloggers' sites. This means you create campaigns that target precisely those bloggers.

- You can ask the bloggers to talk about you, but generally they won't. However, you can place your banner ads on their site. Since your ads include the topics that they're discussing, your ads are relevant to their site, which ensures that you can get placement in the top influencers' blogs.

- You must also use remarketing. When people click on your ad and come to your site, you'll be able to show them additional ads.

Banner ads often have low click rates. You can show 100,000 ads and get only a few hundred clicks. This is okay for two reasons.

- You're paying by the click, not the impression. All of those impressions are free displays of your brand.

- Those unclicked ads actually bring clicks. Remember that people don't want to talk with a sales team? They see the ads, wonder what they're about, and they'll search for the words in the ad, the organization's name, or URL. That's right. You show the ad and people will come to your site without clicking the ad.

I tested this. I took a page that had two years of steady traffic and launched a banner ad campaign (banner ads in seven sizes, close up color photo of the product, strong message, and a strong call-to-action). I showed 250,000 ads in 30 days. The ad got 214 clicks. However, *non-paid traffic went up an additional 621 clicks.* Traffic increased by triple over the paid clicks, just by showing the banner ads.

A few weeks later, we were at a meeting with Google. They told us they had tested banner ads for a mid-sized company and found a large banner ad campaign can produce a 298% increase in traffic. That's the same as my test.

Several of my friends want me to tell you what I tested. Oh, okay. It was my cat. I showed 250,000 ads for my cat's web page. I spent US$12 on the test. I used my cat because I knew there were no other factors to influence the cat's web traffic. No other divisions were running ad campaigns for the cat; she wasn't being interviewed that week in *Fortune*. She was just napping on the sofa. Any increase in traffic was due solely to the banner ads.

Try this for your organization and see what happens.

You're wondering: okay, 250,000 ads for a cat. What about something serious? How about MIT? I manage the PPC campaign for MIT OpenCourseWare project (MIT OCW) . The Google Foundation gave MIT a million dollars in grant money which I use for the online advertising.

The project has 48,000 keywords for MIT's 38 academic subjects in 1,600 courses, such as nuclear engineering, aeronautics, chemistry, computer science, mathematics, and philosophy. I created ads in 14 languages, including Arabic, Russian, and Korean for many parts of the world, including Southeast Asia, the Arab world, and Africa.

Teachers, not students, are the audience. If professors, university lecturers, teachers, tutors, and instructors learn about MIT OCW, they will use it throughout their teaching career and pass it on to other instructors and students. By reaching one instructor, I reach perhaps 1,000 students over the instructor's lifetime.

I've been running the MIT project since 2005. Over 450 million ads have been shown. It has brought 10.1 million visitors. The average CPC is US$0.09 (yes, that's right: I compete against Harvard and Stanford and pay only nine cents for the click). Over four million people have downloaded MIT courses. Of those, tens of thousands around the world go on to have careers as scientists, engineers, and doctors.

The massive number of ads makes people aware of MIT OCW. Eventually, they come to the site, whether they clicked on an ad or not. MIT OCW's acknowledgement page thanks three people: Google, the United Nations, and andreas.com.

7.11. Ad Distribution Services

Google is a search engine, but Google earns its money as an ad distribution service. Google places ads across a network of several million websites. That's how Google makes 98% of their US$50 billion in annual revenues. GMail, Google Maps, Youtube, Android, and the other Google services are just ways to get you to see their ads.

To learn how this works, I signed up Google Adsense to place ads on my website. Google ads have been on my website since 2005. When you come to my site and look at a page about server technology, there may be an ad from Rackspace. If you click the ad, Rackspace pays perhaps US$5 to Google for the click. Google gives about 30% (US$1.50) to me.

(If you're thinking of setting up a blog to get rich on ads, you can expect on average about half a penny (US$0.0066) for every visitor. Instead of CPM, you call it RPM (Revenue per Mille), which tells you how much you get for every 1,000 visitors. This means I get $6.60 RPM from Google. If you have 10,000 monthly readers, you'll earn US$66. You'll need about a million monthly visitors to quit your job. Those "get rich with blogging" articles are nonsense).

If you're wondering how much the big sites earn on advertising, Google Adplanner shows traffic at the 1,000 largest sites. CBS.com, for example, had 5.6 million monthly visitors in 2011, which means they were earning in the high US$36,000s. (You can download the list at my Resources page.)

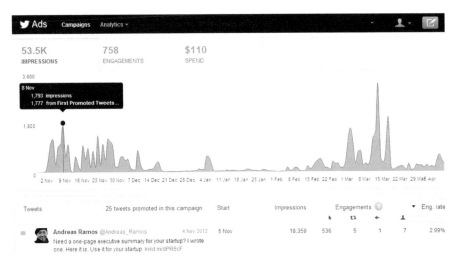

Figure 25: *My ad campaign on Twitter promotes several of my tweets. One tweet was shown 18,359 times, clicked by 536 people, had a 2.99% CTR, and cost US$56.99, or US$0.11 per click, which is quite good compared to other PPC services.*

Google isn't the only ad distribution service. Others include (alphabetically): AOL Advertising, Blogads, Chitika, DoubleClick, Federated Media, Google Ad-Words, Marchex, MediaWhiz, Microsoft Advertising (Bing), OpenX Market, Se-quentialMedia, ValueClick Media, and Yahoo!.

The smaller services generally perform better because they focus on high-traffic, high-value markets. For example, if you want to advertise in travel sites, the small services have identified the top travel sites and pay them more than Google, so your ads will appear on those sites.

In addition, the small services also do everything for you. With Google, you have to do the work: find the keywords, write the ads, manage the bids, and so on. The small ad services ask you for a copy of your Google account. (They show you how to download this). You give it to them and they set up everything. Their teams find more keywords, write new ads, and so on. You negotiate with them on how much you'll pay. For example, you agree to pay US$45 per lead with a cap of 400 leads per month. They do the work, you get the leads, and you pay the bill.

Start with Google. Test this for several months until you find your keywords and best ads. Talk with the other services. Don't use just one or two ad services. I work with most of them.

7.12. Ads in Twitter, LinkedIn, and Facebook

You can also advertise on social sites, including Twitter, LinkedIn, and Facebook.

You can pay for your tweets to be shown on Twitter. As you can see in my example, click rates are fairly high at a low CPC. You can embed tracking tags in the URLs.

LinkedIn lets you target by job title, company, location, or other criteria. For example, you can show ads that appear only to directors and VPs of finance at General Motors. LinkedIn can be very effective. I built a campaign for a mid-range accounting package that produced more sales in one month than the entire previous year.

As everyone knows, there is also advertising on Facebook. Several agencies have told me they've been successful with Facebook advertising for clients. Try a small budget and see if it works for you.

7.13. StumbleUpon

StumbleUpon calls itself a discovery engine. You select one of some 500 topics (astronomy, food, and so on) and it shows you pages in that topic. You can vote if you like or dislike the page. With 25 million members and over 40 billion votes, it has gotten pretty good at showing pages that you'll find interesting.

If you have useful content, people will vote it up and others will see it. If you submit pages that aren't good, people will vote those pages down. Since pages appear at random, a team can't game the system with fake votes (which often happens at Facebook or Digg).

Does this work? Oddly enough, StumbleUpon sends more traffic to my website than Facebook, Twitter, or LinkedIn *combined* (I know this from my web analytics traffic data). Look at your web analytics and see which sites are sending traffic. If you have pages with content that fit in StumbleUpon categories, it might work for you.

StumbleUpon also has a paid service, where you can pay to have your page displayed. Up to 5% of pages may be paid-display pages. You don't create an ad for StumbleUpon. Instead, your page itself is what visitors will see. If you make a blatantly commercial page ("Buy vitamins now!"), people will vote your page down.

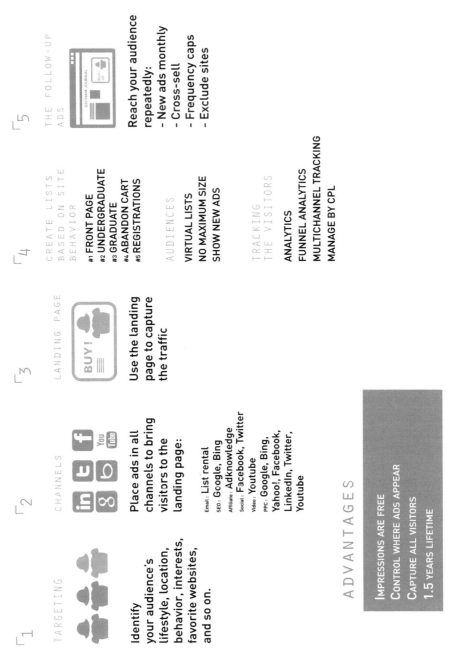

TARGETING

⌐1

Identify your audience's lifestyle, location, behavior, interests, favorite websites, and so on.

CHANNELS

⌐2

Place ads in all channels to bring visitors to the landing page:

Email: List rental
SEO: Google, Bing
Affiliate: Adknowledge
Social: Facebook, Twitter
Video: Youtube
PPC: Google, Bing, Yahoo!, Facebook, LinkedIn, Twitter, Youtube

LANDING PAGE

⌐3

BUY!

Use the landing page to capture the traffic

CREATE LISTS BASED ON SITE BEHAVIOR

⌐4

#1 FRONT PAGE
#2 UNDERGRADUATE
#3 GRADUATE
#4 ABANDON CART
#5 REGISTRATIONS

AUDIENCES

VIRTUAL LISTS
NO MAXIMUM SIZE
SHOW NEW ADS

TRACKING THE VISITORS

ANALYTICS
FUNNEL ANALYTICS
MULTICHANNEL TRACKING
MANAGE BY CPL

THE FOLLOW-UP ADS

⌐5

GOTHAM JOURNAL
BUY

Reach your audience repeatedly:
- New ads monthly
- Cross-sell
- Frequency caps
- Exclude sites

ADVANTAGES

IMPRESSIONS ARE FREE
CONTROL WHERE ADS APPEAR
CAPTURE ALL VISITORS
1.5 YEARS LIFETIME

Figure 26: *An overview of a remarketing campaign.*

I suggest you try this. You can track the results to see if it works for you. Go to StumbleUpon's Paid Discovery (PD) at StumbleUpon.com/pd/.

7.14. Remarketing and Retargeting for Content Marketing

Have you noticed that if you look for a teapot on Amazon, you'll start to see teapots wherever you go on the web for the next few weeks? That's done with *remarketing*.

Remarketing, retargeting, and behavioral retargeting are different names for the same thing. Google calls it remarketing, so I use their term.

Let's say you're thinking about buying something to make tea. Should you get a teapot in glass, ceramic, or iron? What about a Yixing teapot? A cloth filter or wire mesh? Chinese, Japanese, or English? You look around and find Zhihong's site A-Cup-of-Tea.com. She wrote reviews of her collection of 118 teapots. When you go to her website, a Google cookie is placed on your computer. Two days later, you go to the food section of your favorite website. It looks at your computer, sends the cookie to Google, Google looks up your past behavior, and Google places an ad for teapots from A-Cup-of-Tea.com at the top of the news page. You recognize the ad because of the logo (a bird splashing around in a cup of tea). Over the next few weeks, you'll see more ads from A-Cup-of-Tea.com that offer articles on how to clean teapots, comparison of the cost-of-ownership, and special offers. From the various articles, you realize her company has the best products and service, so you're likely to buy from her.

That's remarketing. The ads follow you around the web. Remarketing has the highest conversion rate of any form of digital advertising. According to an IBM Coremetrics white paper, remarketing has 6.8% conversion rate compared to 2.8% for non-remarketing ads. Remarketing produces 2.68 times more revenue than non-remarketing ads. We've seen similar improvements in a number of remarketing campaigns.

Here are several tips for your remarketing campaign:

- Use more than one ad. It's a bit of work, but you should develop remarketing campaigns for each product. For example, A-Cup-of-Tea.com should show different ads to people who visit the different pages for the types of teapots. Those who look at iron teapots should see ads for iron teapots; those who look at ceramic teapots see ads for ceramic teapots.

- When the visitor buys, the cookie changes the visitor's status from shopper to buyer. The teapot ads stop. A new set of ads start for additional products, such as filters and tea.

- You can set a frequency cap so your ads will show three times per day to a person but not more. Most companies don't set this and the endless ads annoy customers.

- You can also set a start and end date. For example, ads can start two days after a visit and turn off after two weeks. Look at your sales cycle. If you see that customers buy within two weeks, there's no point in showing ads for three months.

- You can easily switch ads. You can show ads for summer, winter, and events such as the Olympics.

- You pay only for the click, so it's free to show ads. If your goal is awareness and top-of-mind presence, you can show ads to someone for up to a year and a half.

You can see how remarketing fits into content marketing. You can create ad campaigns that support the different phases of the buying funnel. When visitors come to a page for the awareness phase, they get cookied and then see ads to prompt them to come back to the research phase for white papers, comparisons, and so on. All of your web pages can have remarketing campaigns built around them.

7.15. Which Works Better? Content Marketing or PPC?

You may wonder which works better: content marketing or PPC?

Kapost released *Content Marketing ROI*, a free ebook, which argues content marketing has a more long-term lead and revenue potential than PPC. Here's an example:

- Let's say you spend $1,000 in PPC. The campaign lasts a month. Once the PPC budget has been spent, it's over and the ads no longer appear. Let's say it produced 10 sales, so that's $100 cost-per-action ($1,000 divided by ten sales = $100 CPA).

- You also spend $1,000 on content marketing (for example, you pay a writer and an illustrator to write an article). You post the article to your website. Let's assume it gets a sale every month. In contrast to PPC, the article stays on the web and continues to get traffic every month. After 12 months, the article has gotten 12 sales, so the CPA is now $83.33. After another 12 months, there are 24 sales and the CPA has dropped to $41.66.

An article can exist for five years or more. Some product pages are short-lived, but many content marketing items, such as research, comparisons, and so on have a longer shelf life. I have pages at my website that have been on the web since 1996 and still get several thousand monthly visits. If you use serial publication, you can build an audience that continues for decades.

This is why I think content marketing works better than marketing based on advertising. Ad-based marketing can't match the long-term advantage of content marketing.

On the other hand, advertising has the advantage of quick results. You can launch a nationwide campaign and reach most of your audience within days. Content marketing will take months for people to slowly discover your campaign.

7.16. Don't Turn Off the PPC Ads

I've read a number of content marketing articles where the company develops content marketing, gets lots of business, and gloats that they don't have to pay for advertising. This is just like those companies that do well in SEO and turn off their advertising.

That's a serious mistake. If you know your KPIs, you can show your advertising is making money. If you put in $100 and you get back $200, why would you turn that off? Your advertising is producing additional leads and sales.

If you still want to turn off your advertising, talk with your CFO. Show her this section. She'll straighten you out.

7.17. A Case Study for Content Marketing

There are currently (May 2013) no case studies for content marketing. I've talked with Eloqua, Marketo, Kapost, and most of the authors of the leading books on content marketing. They have client success stories, but they don't have case studies. I've asked Wall Street analysts who follow the leading companies. I've looked at dozens of content marketing case studies. These generally lack sufficient data for statistical significance or control groups.

I'm collecting data for a valid case study, which I'll release at this book's Resources page. Sign up for the newsletter and you'll be notified.

7.18. How to Write a Case Study

A case study is a metrics-driven argument which is used to justify investment. You can present a case study to upper management to get funding for your projects. It shows if you do A, you will get B. For a case study to be valid, it should have the elements listed in table 5.

What to Do	What to Say	Explanation
State the campaign costs	"The test campaign spent $32,000 over 45 days."	Why state the cost and time of the campaign? So others can see if the case study is relevant to their situation. You can't compare a campaign that spent $1,000 over one month to one that spent $2 million in six months.
Describe the tests	"We used A/B split tests as follows. We used multivariate testing as follows."	Why describe the testing? This shows you have strong ads for the case study. For example, you can say "Before we started the campaign, we tested 12 ads and selected the best performer for the case study." Otherwise, skeptics will say low results were due to poor ads.
Describe the tracking	"We used web analytics to track views, clicks, leads, and conversions."	Why describe the tracking process? So readers can see if the authors know what they're doing.
State the results	"30,000 leads converted into 10,000 sales, which is a 33% conversion rate."	Why state the number of conversions and the conversion rate? It's easy to get 100,000 leads with a free giveaway in Facebook, but that will produce very few leads. What counts are the qualified leads.
Use statistically reliable data sets	"We polled 1,100 shoppers and 250 bought the product, so we predict a 22.7% sales rate."	Why more than 1,000? If the data set is too small, the range of confidence for the results will be too wide. You need to poll 1,067 people to get results with a ± 3% range of confidence. If you increase the survey to 2,401 people, the margin of error reduces to ± 2%. For more, see the Wikipedia article on the margin of error.
Describe the control group	"We selected ten US cities with similar demographics. We ran the campaign in seven cities (A, B, C,...). We ran no campaign in three cities (K, L, M). This chart shows the difference in response between the two groups. In test cities, results changed by X. In the control group, results changed by Y."	Why use a control group? If there is no control, there is no proof that the campaign had any effect. The study can conclude "The campaign produced a 12% increase in sales." A skeptic could point out that another division released a new product that got attention, so your increase is due to the other product. Or perhaps your major competitors didn't release new products that quarter, so your increase is due to lack of competition. Worse yet: did the market and your competitors grow 16% last quarter, so your campaign's 12% success is actually a failure? (For a list of control cities, see the metrics chapter).

Table 5: *Elements for a case study.*

When you present a case study, include these elements. If upper management, the board, the investors, or the CFO have proper training in engineering, the sciences, or finances, they will look for statistics and control groups.

When you look at a case study, see if it includes these elements. That'll help you to read the case study critically. A case study that lacks these points is just an anecdote. An anecdote can mislead you either to do something ("It worked for them, so we should do it!") or not do something ("It didn't work for them, so we shouldn't do it.")

To design a case study, you'll need statistically-reliable data. Use NewSurveyShows.com, a free tool that lets you easily calculate how many people to poll and evaluate the reliability of your results.

7.19. Beyond Digital: Off-Page Marketing and Traditional Advertising

I tend to focus on digital marketing because it's easy to track. But with a bit of creativity, you can track other forms of marketing.

Marketing in the 1950s used "above the line" (ATL) and "below the line" (BTL) to determine how to bill for advertising work. For example, ATL included the placement of ads in TV, so the agency billed a percentage of the advertising budget. BTL included activities such as PR, which the agency billed at a flat fee instead of a percentage.

Over time, this distinction blurred into a metaphor and ATL meant mass media and BTL was tactics. But in recent years, the distinction between online and offline (or digital versus traditional) marketing has disappeared. Some now talk of "through the line" (TTL), which means marketing that crosses both ATL and BTL. That is another way of saying "integrated communication marketing" (IMC).

The need to punch through the audience's blindness to advertising has pushed ad agencies to creative extremes. Many clever ads use funny or remarkable events, stunts, buzz marketing, or guerilla marketing. The low point was a Super Bowl ad in which a hamster was shot out of a cannon.

There are also campaigns that cut across different formats. For example, some TV campaigns send people to a YouTube video, which in turn gets people to scan bus signs and see animated monsters. This type of advertising is possible because digital tools such as QR codes and NFC have extended links into the real world.

Figure 27: *Use your cell phone to scan the QR code to see a video or an app.*

You can use QR codes and NFC tags to create links that can be printed on items such as T-shirts, shopping bags, and billboards or storefront advertising. QR codes are squares of little dots (pictured above). NFC tabs are little stickers.

Both QR codes and NFC tags can contain links URLs and telephone numbers. They can also include PayPal payment links (where you scan the code to make a payment), links to a video, an email address with text, or an SMS messages.

People can use their phone cameras to scan a QR square or pass their phone over the NFC tag. This scans the tag and a web page opens or an SMS is sent.

You can embed tracking code into the URL so when people scan the QR or NFC tag, their action is recorded in your web analytics. This means real-world transactions, conversions, and sales can be tracked in your web analytics.

A number of advertisers are trying to update their business model by developing offline tracking that matches online tracking. They do this by connecting the traditional advertising on the "first screen" (the TV screen) to the "second screens" (such as cell phones, tablets, and laptop computers) to measure the impact of the ad. In 2011, Old Navy had launched a video campaign on TV, Radio, Facebook, and YouTube in collaboration with Shazam, a website for music and videos. Each ad was a 30-second video clip that was connected to a song. The taggers could buy the music via iTunes and the clothes at the store.

There was a coupon for the first 1,000 people who tagged the ad.

- 70% of the first 1,000 used their coupon
- More than 150,000 people tagged the songs
- 31,000 persons bought additional items (music or clothes) after tagging the video
- One of the songs promoted by Old Navy was the most tagged song at Shazam for the month

Make sure the stuff you hand out is useful. If your audience is health-conscious, put your QR or NFC tags on 100,000 pedometers and tell people they can scan these to visit a website where they can track their BMI, health, and fitness. Think about what your audience finds really useful. Content isn't just what they read. It can also include useful things.

Oasis, a French fruit drink, created a brand personality by using content marketing. Their Unique Value Proposition is "Only Water & Fruits." Their content marketing strategy is to create fruit characters with different personalities and tell the story of the fruits, living in our world, through real and fictional events with stories, photos, and videos. These include Cactus Kid on the run with his girlfriend or RubberDuckZilla, who attacks Tokyo. (It's a pretty crazy commercial. Watch it on YouTube.) To build upon the idea of fun and natural fruit drinks, Oasis set up a summer amusement park. The constant flow of content built awareness and loyalty among 12-25 year-olds.

7.20. Summary of this Chapter

Advertising has its place as a tactic in a content marketing strategy. You can rapidly create awareness and drive traffic to a new product or service. An advertising campaign based on targeted banner ads can reach most of your audience within days. In contrast, content marketing can take weeks or months to reach the same level of penetration into your market. However, content marketing has the advantage over the long term. The cost of hosting and distributing the content is nearly zero.

Finally, if advertising is managed to CPL and CPA, you can show that it is profitable and produces additional leads and sales.

Off-Page Marketing? How about Off-World Marketing?

Red Bull's Jump from Space with Felix Baumgartner was the biggest marketing stunt of the last 20-30 years. Baumgartner jumped from a balloon at the edge of space.

Red Bull broadcasted the live event via YouTube for 2.5 hours worldwide without paying anything to TV. They had complete control (no network TV moderators, journalists, delayed broadcast, interruptions, or commercials). The jump's live audience was a third of the size of the Super Bowl audience; the total audience was over 366 million views on YouTube alone.

This wasn't a one-time event. Red Bull hosts an ongoing series of games and extreme sports as serial content marketing which now produce as much revenue as the drinks.

REDBULL

CONTENT GALAXY

MOTORSPORTS

SPONSORING

BIKE

EVENT ORGANIZER

GAMES

SPORTSMEN ENDORSEMENT

MUSIC LABEL

SURFING

GAME DESIGNER

MUSIC

SNOWBOARDING

DISTRIBUTION CHANNELS

20+ CHANNELS
692 000+ SUSCRIBERS
2000+ PHOTOS

20+ CHANNELS
2M+ FOLLOWERS
45 000+ TWEETS

20+ CHANNELS
37M+ FANS

10+ CHANNELS
700M+ VIEWS
2.6M+ SUSCRIBERS
3 000+ VIDEOS

4 CHANNELS
2.3M+ FANS

WWW.
25+ CHANNELS

8. Tracking, Metrics, and Business Goals

8.1. What's in This Chapter

The point of any business strategy or tactic is to support the organization's business goals. Those goals are measured by top-line and bottom-line business metrics. The combination of digital technology, Web 1.0, Web 2.0, marketing automation, and CRM enables tracking of all activity (visits, leads, costs, sales, revenue) from "click to close," which means you can finally turn marketing into a measurable activity that supports business goals.

Metrics have profound implications in marketing. These allow you to measure, manage, and improve your marketing projects as they are in progress. You can create a digital marketing platform that actively drives revenue and profits. You can prove how much you contributed to revenue.

8.2. The Purpose of Metrics-Based Marketing

Over the last hundred years, every area of business has adopted the scientific method to decision making. Engineering, production, transportation, distribution, finance, and HR use evidence-based decision making to produce the best results.

The ideas are simple. Set a measurable goal. Use testing to collect objective data and measure results. Eliminate weak processes. Create variations of a good process to find even better processes. The result is the optimal solution.

Many technology companies are founded by engineers, who apply engineering methods to all aspects of their companies, including marketing. CFOs use data to evaluate results. Investors use metrics to manage investments. They all want to apply metrics to marketing.

This trend towards metrics-based marketing will continue because metrics-based companies have "…significantly better sales growth and financial performance…" (Mark Jeffery, *Data-Driven Marketing*, 2012).

8.3.   Faith-Based Marketing

Some people choose to study marketing because they think it doesn't use numbers. So they call marketing an art, which is another way of saying they don't know how it works. The result is faith-based marketing.

Because CFOs and investors demand metrics, these marketers come up with numbers such as eyeballs, hits, views, impressions, engagement, likes, follows, and similar. Joe Chernov calls these "vanity metrics." Without metrics, there is no way to measure performance towards business goals. They can't measure the impact (positive or negative) on leads, sales, revenues, or costs. Vanity metrics look like numbers but don't measure anything.

Tracking is often a disincentive. A few years ago, a friend suggested to his boss that they start tracking the marketing projects. The VP of marketing said "If you start collecting data, we might be held accountable!"

8.4.   The Use of Metrics in Content Marketing

Here is an overview of a metrics-based marketing strategy.

- Goals are set, which include values and time, such as "increase sales by 10% by December 31st."

- Each item of content (report, white paper, video, and so on) is placed in a phase of the buying funnel: awareness, consideration, or purchase.

- Each content item aims to move the visitor from that phase to the next phase of the buying funnel.

- Metrics tools can measure the number of visitors to each phase and the number of transitions, both successful and unsuccessful (abandonment), to the next phase.

- Use A/B split testing and multivariate testing to test multiple versions of content. Metrics can track the results of different versions. The data can be used to increase what works and decrease (or stop) what doesn't work. Leads and sales will increase.

- Metrics can also measure changes in the speed of the sales cycle and the quality of leads.

This strategy is quite different from faith-based marketing. Some of those campaigns were memorable. Some won awards. That increased the marketer's reputation and salary. However, there was no objective way to measure or evaluate campaigns. Successes were unrepeatable. Failures were ignored. Whether those campaigns contributed to the company's revenues was unknown.

The "Got Milk?" campaign is well-known in the USA. It has been running for twenty years. It has 90% awareness in the US market. It has been voted one of the ten best ad campaigns of all time.

Yet milk consumption is now at the lowest point in three decades and the trend continues down.

8.5.   What to Track and How to Track

You can track the activity on your content: downloads, contacts, movement through the buying funnel, and more. Table 6 (next page) gives an overview of what you can track and how to do it.

I give only a brief summary of how to track. You can find details on how to write the tracking code at many websites. The point is to show it is fairly easy to track.

You can track:

- Channels, such as Facebook, Twitter, Google AdWords, YouTube, email lists, LinkedIn, Pinterest, Instagram, TV ads, post cards, QR codes, NFC tags, and bus signs

- Platforms, such as desktop, tablet, and smart phones

- Actions, including traffic, visitors, clicks, leads, conversions, and sales

- Financial metrics, including cost-per-lead (CPL), cost-per-action (CPA), and revenues

8.6.   Testing with A/B Splits and Multivariate Testing

You can test just about anything: text ads, banner ads, web pages, product colors, and so on. Testing lets you see what happens when you make changes. Which ad works better? What if you change something? You can find what works better. You can also delete whatever doesn't work. Always use data to make decisions.

Where to Track	What to Track	How to Track
Track the links and pages	On-page tracking is the tracking of actions that happens on your own web pages. Web analytics tools reports the visits, exits, clicks, originating site, time-on-site, bounce rate, keywords, actions, registrations, and sales on your website.	Paste several lines of analytics code on the page.
Track events	Off-page tracking is the tracking of activity of your content on other places, such as other web pages and social sites (like Facebook or Twitter). This means you track actions that happen on websites that you don't control. This is done with a new set of analytics tools, such as social analytics, conversation analytics, and so on. You can also track actions on non-web objects, such as postcards, QR codes on shop windows, and so on. You can tag a link so that when someone clicks the link, web analytics registers it as an event. This lets you track action on clicks, such as when someone clicks a link to go to an external site or send you an email, download a file, click a redirects, or uses Flash, video, and so on.	Add JavaScript code to the links or buttons.
Track Links on Other Sites	When you post to Facebook, send out a press release, or distribute a PDF, you include a link that points back to your page. The link includes a tracking tag. This lets you see how many people clicked those links. You can also use unique IDs for each link so you can see which ones were clicked. For example, you can see that you got 400 clicks at Facebook, 500 from your press release, and 200 from the PDF. Conversions can be tied to these so you know Facebook produced 100 sales and the PDF produced 50.	Add tracking tag to the links. Use unique IDs to identify the links. Use a URL shortening service (such as Bit.ly) to shorten and encrypt the link.
Track Pages as Goal Conversions	You can track pages as a goal. When a visitor goes through the shopping process and reaches the thank-you page (the conversion page), that counts as a conversion. You can either assign a conversion value (for example, $100) or capture the value from the shopping cart (for example, $124.32).	Paste several lines of web analytics code on the page. Configure the analytics tool to recognize the thank-you page's URL as the conversion page.
Track Events as Goal Conversions	You can also track events as a goal. For example, a registration can be a goal. You can also assign a conversion value (for example, $100).	Configure the analytics tool to recognize the event as a conversion event.
Track the Funnel	Funnel analysis lets you track how many people enter a sales funnel, how many exit at each phase, and how many move to the next phase. This also lets you see how much loss there is in each phase so you can test to make improvements. It can also measure the velocity or time length of the sales cycle.	Configure the analytics tool to track the URLs of each stage of the sales funnel.

Table 6: *What to track and how to do it.*

There are two kinds of tests:

- **A/B Split Testing:** This is a basic test and easy to carry out. Which works better? An ad with a summer or a winter background? A family or a couple? Instead of using opinions (or generally deferring to the person with the most seniority), you can test. Compare the results.

- **Multivariate Testing:** This allows you to test many versions at the same time to find the best combination. Let's say you want to make the best-possible landing page so you test four headlines, three photos, five body texts, and three call-to-action buttons. That's 180 combinations (4 x 3 x 5 x 3 = 180). With a multivariate testing tool, you can easily create all of these combinations and test them to find the best combination. As the test is going on, you'll quickly see that some combinations are weak and can be turned off. Google offers a free multivariate testing tool as part of Google Analytics.

When the test ends, you're ready to start the next round. Look at the best results from your test and make new versions of ads or landing pages based on those results. If you find that a photo of a couple works better than one of a family, try new ads with the couple on the right side or the left side. Try different clothes on the people.

When I first started testing, I found that switching two words could result in a 2% difference in conversions. I tested all sorts of variations to end up with ads and landing pages with very high conversion rates.

All of your campaigns must include testing. This lets you be certain that you're using the best ads and landing pages.

8.7.   You Can't Fail a Test

When Thomas Edison was developing the light bulb, he tried over 3,000 filaments until he found the right one. A reporter asked him what it was like to fail 3,000 times. Edison replied "I didn't fail once. I found 3,000 ways in which it doesn't work."

When you test, you don't have failure. You have proof something didn't work. Keep track of your tests so you don't have to repeat them.

8.8.   Four out of Ten Dentists Agree

You'll never get easy numbers in your tests. It's always odd numbers such as 1,321 with 342 clicks (25.9%) or 2,471 with 684 clicks (27.7%). Is 27.7% better than 25.9%? Is that due to the larger sample? Or is that just within the range of random difference?

An easy tool lets you compare statistical results and see if the difference is real or just random. Go to NewSurveyShows.com, enter your numbers, and press Calculate. Try the numbers in the previous paragraph and see if there is a difference or not.

8.9.   US Cities as Test Markets

If you know the demographic parameters for a country (such as age, sex, education, income, and location), you can look for cities with the same percentages and use them as test markets. For example, Hispanics make up 16.7% of the United States population, so you can look for cities with 16.7% Hispanics.

This means you can test a product by using one city instead of the entire US.Here is a list of US cities whose demographics match the general US population:

- Albany-Schenectady-Troy, New York
- Birmingham, Alabama
- Cedar Rapids, Iowa
- Charlotte-Gastonia-Rock Hill, North Carolina / South Carolina
- Columbus, Ohio
- Eau Claire, Wisconsin
- Eugene-Springfield, Oregon
- Grand Junction, Colorado
- Greensboro--Winston-Salem--High Point, North Carolina
- Nashville, Tennessee
- Odessa-Midland, Texas
- Pittsfield, Massachusetts
- Richmond-Petersburg, Virginia
- Rochester, New York
- Syracuse, New York
- Wichita, Kansas
- Wichita Falls, Texas

How do you use this list? Prepare two marketing campaigns. Launch campaign A in six cities and campaign B in six additional cities. The remaining cities are the control group, in other words, you do no marketing in those cities. Place bets in your office, collect data, and compare the results. You'll see if the campaigns work.

8.10. Web Analytics

The major web analytics tools are Webtrends, Adobe Omniture, IBM Coremetrics, and Google Analytics. Google Analytics has an 80% market share.

A secret in web analytics is that most of the data is ignored. Only a few analytics reports actually matter: the keywords, pages with the most incoming visitors, referring sites, geographic location, bounce rates, and the ratio of desktop to mobile users. The webmaster uses web analytics to monitor pages and make changes. Upper management looks only at data that affects KPIs.

The analytics space is undergoing evolution as people move away from the simple model of desktop computers, websites, and search engines. New types of analytics companies offer social analytics, mobile analytics, app analytics, comment analytics, and so on.

Which should you use? Try several of these tools. Look at your data from different angles and see what works for you.

- **Predictive Analytics:** Uses statistics, modeling, and data mining to find patterns to identify risks and opportunities. It discovers relationships among many factors. Predictive analytics is entirely different from web analytics.

- **Web Analytics:** Presents past data (traffic, clicks, and keywords) of traffic to web pages. The data is generally used to improve the website.

- **Sentiment Analytics:** Show trends and sentiment (positive, neutral, negative) of engagement. It also compares organizations. (Also called comment analytics or social analytics).

- **Mobile Analytics:** Analytics for mobile devices. Along with page views, it shows location, device type, screen resolution, service provider, language, and so on.

- **App Analytics:** Shows the use of an app: the number of downloads, installs, uninstalls, frequency of use, time-on-app, and more.

- **Influencer Analytics:** Identifies influencers and ranks them by size of audience, frequency of posting, relevance of postings, sentiment, ranking, and more. Some of these also show word clouds or lists of topics. Advanced versions can manage your conversation with influencers.

Here's an example of an influencer analytics tool: EzyInsights.com is a combination of conversation monitor and influencer marketing. You can see which postings provoke the most comments, likes, and shares. You can also see a list of

Figure 28: *A word cloud shows the conversation topics in a social forum. You can use EzyInsights to create word clouds for the postings by a single person.*

the people who are actively engaging with you. You can rank them by activity to see which person gets the most comments by others about you, which means you know who the influencers are. EzyInsights shows word clouds for the cumulative conversation (what everyone is saying) along with a word cloud for each influencer (you can see what the influencer is saying). You can also use this to monitor the conversations around your competitors.

Your goal is to identify your valuable brand ambassadors. They're enthusiastically talking about you to their followers. You can strengthen the relationship to your ambassadors by working with them. Give them advanced notice of new products, give them special access to your developers and management, and feature them in your newsletter and marketing.

Several years ago, Anastasia worked on a campaign for a global watch company. She looked into the company's followers and found a woman in Vancouver who was very passionate about the watches. When the woman heard a new model was coming out, she'd go to the mall and wait for hours to be the first one to have it. She'd take it home, take photos from all angles, and write several long blog postings about it. The company had no idea she was doing this. So Anastasia contacted her and asked her if she'd like to get the new watches delivered to her by express mail before the release date. The woman became the company's unofficial expert in the watches.

Find your fans and work with them. They're already out there.

You've now seen how the various tools collect data. The next step is to apply that data to a goal.

The goals are measured with *Key Performance Indicators* (KPIs). As the name implies, these are the important numbers that show what is happening. KPIs are the metrics that measure your organization's business goals.

There are lots of things that you can measure, but I focus only on business goals. Why? Because business goals are the purpose of the organization. The board and management set the business goals and use a handful of metrics to measure and manage the organization. These metrics include revenue, units, length of sales cycle, inventory turnover, and profits. These metrics determine careers, compensation, and bonuses.

Investors want to maximize their investment. They look at dozens (or hundreds) of companies in a market space and sort them by financial metrics. Companies with top KPIs will get investments. Companies that underperform won't get investment and won't last long.

These metrics are presented in three standard business documents: the balance sheet (a summary of liabilities and assets), the income statement (a summary of revenues and expenses), and the cash-flow statement.

There are two kinds of KPIs: top-line and bottom-line. The names come from the place where the numbers appear on the company's income statement (a one-page summary of the business).

- **Top-line KPIs:** At the top of the income statement, the first line (the top line) states the company's total revenues (how much was sold).

- **Bottom-line KPIs:** At the bottom of the income statement, the last line (in other words, the bottom line) states the company's profits, (how much money was earned). When you take revenues and deduct the expenses and taxes, what's left is the profit (which is usually called earnings or net income).

To put it simply, top-line is how much money came in and bottom-line is the profits. Whether it's IBM or your mom's cookie shop in Bangalore, it comes down to a few basic numbers.

If you report numbers that aren't part of these business metrics, your report will be ignored at the upper levels. CFOs don't care about social media likes because these can't be tied to revenue. If you report metrics that matter to upper management, you'll get attention, you'll get budget, and you'll move up.

It really is all about the numbers. Wendy Chang and I are working on building a Silicon Valley startup. We often go to pitch events in Palo Alto, where startup teams present their projects to investors. We see this over and over: investors discuss only the financials. How much will be invested? How will it spent? What are the metrics?

A few years ago, we had a new marketing intern. I asked him why he chose marketing. He said it was because he hated math and there was no math in marketing. I didn't say anything. An hour later, I said "okay, now I'll show you how to calculate CPLs."

8.12. Top-Line and Bottom-Line as Goals

Numbers become useful when you use them to set goals and measure progress towards those goals.

- **The top-line KPI is revenue**. You can break this down into the number of leads, the number of units sold, and the price. By making projections, you can make a good guess at the future. By tracking the data, you can test and adjust to reach those goals.

- **The bottom-line KPI is profit (net income).** This can also be broken down into costs and length of the sales cycle. By lowering costs, you can increase profits. By reducing the length of the sales cycle, you can sell more, which increases profits.

These numbers become even more useful when you use them to justify investments.

- If you can show that a $100,000 marketing budget produced $250,000 in revenues last quarter, then you can argue that $200,000 will produce $500,000 next quarter. Your marketing budget isn't a cost; it becomes an investment.

- If you can show how reductions in costs will improve profits, you can justify the reductions, instead of making random budget cuts that start political battles.

Don't just state a number ("sales were $250,000.") You should always state the amount of change, the percentage, and the time span. State the change ("sales went from $200,000 to $250,000, which is an increase of $50,000"), the percentage of change ("sales increased 20%,") and the time span ("this quarter compared to last quarter") to allow meaningful comparison.

If you see a report that lacks several numbers, it usually means someone doesn't know how to report the numbers, has a poor strategy, or is hiding bad news.

So how do you use these KPIs? Here are examples of usage:

The Change	Type of KPI	What It Shows
Number of Leads	Top Line	Leads went from 600 to 720, an increase of 120 leads (120%) over last quarter. More sales and profits can be expected.
Sales in Units	Top Line	Sales of units went from 600 to 630, an increase of 30 units (105%) over last quarter. Revenues and profits will increase.
Revenues	Top Line	Revenues went from $150,000 to $250,000, an increase of $100,000 (167%) over last quarter.
Costs	Bottom Line	Costs dropped from $120,000 to $100,000, a decrease of $20,000 (17%) over last quarter. By lowering costs (and if revenues stay the same), profits increase by $20,000.
Profits	Bottom Line	Profits went from $75,000 to $100,000, an increase of $25,000 (133%) over last quarter.
Length of Sales Cycle	Bottom Line	The average length of the sales cycle went from 67 days to 59 days, a decrease of 8 days (12%) over last quarter. A shorter sales cycle means more units are sold.

Table 7:   *KPIs: Top LIne and Bottom Line, and how to use them.*

8.14. Content Marketing and KPIs: Investor Dashboard

Let's now connect the KPIs to content marketing, the subject of this book.

Here's a simplified table for the KPIs:

Title	Budget	Visits	Leads	CPL	Sales	CPA
Doc 001	$100	209	34	$2.94	16	$6.25
Doc 002	$250	1,512	292	$0.86	143	$1.75
Doc 003	$125	753	164	$0.76	92	$1.36
Total	$475	2,474	490	$0.97	251	$1.89

Table 8: *The investor Dashboard.*

Note: These numbers are examples. Because the page is small, I show only a few columns in the table. Get the spreadsheet at the book's Resources page.

The table shows the budget for each channel (for example, a $250 budget for a blog posting), the visits (1,512 views), the leads (292 visitors turned into leads), the cost-per-lead ($250/292 leads = $0.86 CPL), and the cost-per-action ($250/142 sales = $1.76 CPA).

You can add details, such as cost-per-click (CPC), click-through-rates (CTR), change, and so on.

The important number is the total CPA (cost-per-action) at the bottom right ($1.89). If the campaign CPA is within the maximum CPA, your campaign is profitable. As long as you stay within the campaign CPA, you can increase the budget and profits will increase.

If your campaign exceeds the maximum CPA, you must bring the metrics under control. Do this by improving the tactics that have high CPAs. In the table above, you can start with the first account.

But don't rest with fixing a few tactics. If you improve every tactic, your overall CPA goes down, which gives you more profits. Carry out tests on every tactic, every ad, and every landing page. I'm often asked about the conversion rate. What's the average conversion rate? That's like asking for the average speed of all Brazilians in the 100 meter race. The national average is pretty bad. What matters are the few Brazilians who are good enough for the Olympics. On average, companies get 1-2% conversion. But that's really low. We've worked with clients who had 17% conversion rates. Some large corporations get 40% conversion rates or higher. (How can it be so high? They have a very strong brand).

To learn how to calculate the maximum CPA, get the KPI ebook at the book's Resources page.

The next step for your spreadsheet is to add the data to the editorial calendar. This lets you track the contribution of each content item to the overall marketing process.

You can also track the length of the sales cycle. You can track leads as they progress through the various stages of the buying funnel (awareness, consideration, and purchase). As you build data and use testing to develop robust content, you can begin to estimate future levels of leads and sales. You can also carry out tests to shorten the sales cycle length, which increases your revenues and profits by allowing more sales in the same time period.

Let's say you've carried out A/B split and multivariate testing for several months and you've developed a series of pretty good pages that move your audience from visit to lead to sale. Let's say 10,000 people come to the website and 6,000 of them go to pages for the awareness phase (and 4,000 exit the website). That's a 60% success rate and a 40% abandon rate. Of those 6,000, about 4,000 go to the set of pages for the consideration phase. Of that number, 1,000 decide to buy (so in the purchase phase, you have 66% success and 33% abandonment). Of the original 10,000 visitors, you have a 10% success rate.

You can now make a pretty good guess that if you double your budget from $10,000 to $20,000, you'll double the visitors to 20,000. The ratio of success/abandon should remain the same (with a ± 2% margin of confidence), so you can expect the same 10% success rate, or around 2,000 customers. Set up your spreadsheet with variables for the budget so you can change the amount to see the impact.

With tracking, you'll know the amount of traffic that comes to the website, how many people register, and how many of those registered visitors turn into customers. With testing, you can improve the flow. After a few months, you'll reach optimal performance. You'll now know that for a budget of $10,000, you produce sales of 1,000 units at $200 per unit. You can then increase the budget to increase the amount of traffic that comes into the funnel, which means you increase the sales. With metrics and testing, you can predict sales and revenues.

When you present your estimates to the CFO, she'll ask how you got them. You can show your data. (Be ready to explain every number! No number is too small for a CFO). Your marketing budget is now an investment that produces sales and revenues.

8.15. Beyond Budgets

This approach goes beyond setting quarterly budgets. This data can be presented as an investor dashboard. A startup can carry out a pilot campaign to collect data. Industry trends and competitor data can be plugged into your model so you can project trends and sales to your investors. If you include variables in your spreadsheet's cells, you can show tables with current results for current budgets and create new tables in which you can enter higher budgets and see the result.

Investors can see that the model works and can project how much investment will be needed to reach goals. What happens if you spend $100,000? What happens if you spend $500,000? Or $2 million?

If you know a CPA is $7.32, then $10,000 will buy you 1,370 sales. $100,000 should buy you 13,700 sales. You buy the number of sales that you need.

You can then turn this around and ask how many sales are needed to be cash-flow positive and then allocate sufficient budget to reach that goal.

8.16. Summary of this Chapter

This chapter shows how a content marketing strategy supports the company's business goals. The goals are stated as numbers and time. Tactics can then be carried out and tested to see if they lead to movement to reach those goals. Weak tactics can be paused. Successful tactics can be relaunched in new variations to find better versions. Metrics turns marketing into an investment.

Closing

"Half the money I spend on advertising is wasted;
the trouble is I don't know which half."

-- John Wanamaker (1838-1922)

Wanamaker's line is probably the most famous quotation in marketing, but it's no longer true.

It's worse than that.

Today, ol' John would say "80% of the money I spend on online advertising doesn't reach its audience" (That 80% is based on research by Tim Suther, CMO, Acxiom, 2012.)

I started this book because I saw marketing was losing its effect. I worked with Fortune 500s and we saw how hard it was to reach our audiences. I also work with startups in Silicon Valley and I saw executives and investors were skeptical of marketing. They were reluctant to allocate marketing budgets because they couldn't see results. I began to look for better solutions.

The digitization of information and Web 1.0 fundamentally undermined the economics of traditional information production and distribution for print, radio, and TV. Web 2.0 gave the controls to the audience. They vote, share, and discuss. Push marketing becomes impossible when the audience can simply walk away. These new tools let us understand what our audience wants. You can use influencer marketing to quickly spread your message at a very low cost.

SEO also changed. Traditional SEO was based on search engines, but the audience has moved to Web 2.0, social media, and text messaging to share and discuss. It's no longer enough to be in the search engines.

Content marketing is the solution to today's digital world. Your audience wants customer-centric content. They are looking for answers to their problems. Give them answers. They will share your content with their friends.

But we're in for more changes. What's coming next?

We've had ten years of Web 2.0 and the dust hasn't settled. The current social media sites have limits. Better social media sites are coming. Yes, much more chaos is coming.

Mobile has arrived. Mobile is now the main way to use the web. Every company will have to restructure for this.

And after that? Remember: marketing and advertising are the running dogs of industrialized production. Marketing exists because there is factory production. Traditional marketing and advertising, which were secondary results of the Industrial Revolution, will also fade. However, production is about to undergo its own digitization. 3D printing allows people to make anything without the need for production, shipping, or stores. 3D printing is disruptive technology that disintermediates the production and distribution chain. What will happen to factories? And marketing and advertising? Interesting times, indeed.

-- Andreas Ramos
Palo Alto
May 13th, 2013

Resources at Andreas.com

Connect to me. I'd love to hear your comments and ideas about content marketing. Visit my website: andreas.com

Resources

You can find free downloads and updates at the book's Resources page at andreas.com/c-m/

I will release a case study and additional tools when these are ready. To be notified, sign up for the newsletter.

If you know useful resources, please let me know at the book's comment box. Do you have something to say? Write in the comments box or email me.

The Deleted Scenes

You know how the Shrek DVD has deleted scenes that were cut from the movie?

Yes, I also have "deleted scenes" from this book. After much discussion, an entire chapter was deleted. Some of the book's advisors liked it, others said it was off topic. Many ideas, notes, comments, and yes, many jokes were deleted. I moved those to the Deleted Scenes page at the book's website.

Contact Me

I release new ebooks and items every few weeks. To be notified, subscribe to my newsletter at the book's Resources page at my website.

- Resources page at andreas.com/c-m/

- Website: andreas.com

Follow me on Facebook or Twitter. Read my blog. Or connect via LinkedIn. For links, go to andreas.com and select Contact.

An invaluable resource is the Content Marketing Institute (CMI), run by . It has links to additional resources, events, and materials.
Go to ContentMarketingInstitute.com

There are a number of useful books on content marketing. Here is are the best ones:

Content Marketing, Rebecca Lieb (Que, 2011).
Website at rebeccalieb.com/blog

Content Rules, Ann Handley (Wiley, 2nd ed., 2012).
Website at ContentRulesBook.com

Content Strategy for the Web, Kristina Halvorson and Melissa Rach (New Riders, 2nd ed. 2012). Website at ContentStrategy.com

Get Content Get Customers, Joe Pulizzi and Newt Barrett (Voyager Media, 2009)

Inbound Marketing, Brian Halligan and Dharmesh Shah (Wiley, 2010).
Website at hubspot.com.

Managing Content Marketing, Robert Rose and Joe Pulizzi (CMI, 2011).

Optimize, Lee Odden (Wiley, 2012).
Website at OptimizeBook.com

Valuable Content Marketing, Sonja Jefferson and Sharon Tanton (Kogan Page, 2013).
Website at ValuableContent.co.uk

Contact the Contributors of this Book:

Alexander Bravo West (alexbravowest@gmail.com)
Antonin Rémond (antonin.remond@mailhec.com)
Daniel Reyes (danrey17@gmail.com)
Jessica Back (edits@jessicabackdesign.net)
Katie Fox (katiefox@gmail.com)
Mathieu Badie (mathieu.badie@betwin.fr)
Michael DeLong (michael.m.delong@gmail.com)
Prudence Hull (prudence.hull@gmail.com)
Robin Goka (robingoka@yahoo.com)
Sandra Truc (sandra.truc@betwin.fr)
Susan Silvius (ssilvius.editing@gmail.com)
Suzana Gorea (suzana.gorea@betwin.fr)
Sydney Pfaff (sydney@sydneypfaff.com)

Glossary

A/B Split Testing   A testing method used in marketing to find which ad performs better. Test two (or more) ads on the same audience and see which ad produces more conversions. See also Multivariate Testing.

Action   A lead converts into a buyer when they perform a defined action. Actions include register an account, subscribe to a newsletter, buy a product, download a PDF, and so on. Every page should have a clear action for the visitor. See Conversion.

Audience   See Target Audience.

Bottom-line KPIs   At the bottom of the income statement, the last line (in other words, the bottom line) states the company's profits, (how much money was earned). When you take revenues and deduct the expenses and taxes, what's left is the profit (which is usually called earnings or net income).

Business model   The business model is how the business makes money. McDonald's makes money by selling hamburgers. When we talk about ideas for new companies in Silicon Valley, one of the first questions is "What's the business model?" Often, the product and the business model aren't the same. Google's product is a search engine, but their business model is advertising. General Motors builds cars, but they make money on car loans and financing.

Call-to-Action   On a page, clearly state to your visitor what you want him to do, such as buy a product, download a PDF, and so on. This is usually written as CTA.

Click-Through Rate (CTR)   If an ad is displayed 100 times and 20 people click on it, that's a 20% CTR.

Close   When you make a sale, you "close" a customer.

Close Rate (CR)   The ratio of how many leads turn into customers. If you have 100 leads and 25 turn into customers, your close rate is 25%. Also called the conversion rate.

Confirmation Page   When a visitor makes a successful conversion (they fill out a form, they buy a product), a confirmation page appears. It says "Your order was successful." You place conversion-tracking code on that page so you can track conversions. This is often called a thank-you page.

Conversion   A conversion is a successful action by a visitor. If a visitor buys a product, they convert from visitor to customer. See Action.

Cost-per-Action (CPA)   The cost for an action (or conversion). Divide the campaign costs by the number of actions to get the CPA.

Cost-per-Click (CPC)   The cost for a click. Divide the campaign costs by the number of clicks to get the CPC.

Cost-per-Lead (CPL)	The cost for a lead. Divide the campaign costs by the number of leads to get the CPL.
Cost-per-Thousand (CPM)	(CPM, where M is thousand in Latin) The cost of an ad measured by blocks of 1000 impressions. For example, if a newspaper ad is shown to 80,000 readers, that's 80 blocks of 1000 readers. CPMs are priced in dollars, such as $2 per CPM.
CTA	See Call-to-Action.
Customer Relations Management (CRM)	Use CRM tools to manage customers to maximize profitability and service. A CRM system contains customer information, such as customer actions, purchase history, and customer preferences.
Disintermediation	This means "to remove the middleman." For example, MP3 players allow people to listen to their favorite 5000 songs without commercials. This cuts the radio stations out of the music, which ends their ability to sell advertising. The Web creates disintermediation because customers can connect directly to manufacturers.
Funnels	Used to track how many people enter a website and then drop out or continue at each step of the conversion process. This is also called scenario analysis or path analysis.
Goals	A goal is a desired action at a website, such as a registration, subscription to a newsletter, purchase of a product, download of a PDF, and so on. See Conversion.
Impressions	An impression is when someone has the opportunity to see your ad. It doesn't mean they actually saw your ad. When you browse through a magazine, each ad gets an impression. Impressions don't indicate much.
Key Performance Indicator(KPI)	The numbers that matter for your business. The top KPIs include top-line and bottom-line numbers.
Keywords	This is the search term that someone enters in a search engine to search for something.
KPI	See Key Performance Indicator.
Landing Page (LP)	The visitor clicks on a link or ad and is brought to a landing page. The landing page is relevant to the visitor's search and offers a clear path to action (lead or purchase).
Lead	Also known as a prospect, a lead is a potential customer.
Lifetime Value	The lifetime value (LTV) is the total value of a customer's purchases over the lifetime of the customer. For many types of products and services, a customer returns again and again to buy more products. Instead of measuring customers by the value of a single sale, consider the lifetime value of a customer as the total profit from all sales.

Multivariate Testing (MVT)	Multivariate testing tools let you create permutations of a page and then test all the versions to find which version performs better. MVT tools are either brute force (they test all versions) or they use Taguchi Method, which tests a subset.
Natural Search	The unpaid results on the left side in search engines. On the right side are the PPC ads (paid placement). Unpaid listings are called organic results, natural results, or algorithmic results.
Organic Search	See Natural Search.
Organization	In this book, I use "organization" as a broad term for companies, corporations, governments, associations, educational organizations, religious groups, clubs, and so on.
Page Views	How many times a web page has been viewed. A page may be viewed 200 times, but you don't know how many people saw it, because one person could have seen it 50 times. Unique visitors are a better number, but that doesn't really matter. What matters is the business goal, such as the number of conversions.
Path Analysis	See Funnels.
Pay-per-Click (PPC)	This is an online advertising model in which you pay for each click on your ad.
PPC	See Pay per Click.
Salience	Something is salient if it stands out from the others in its category. There are lots of running shoes, but Nike stands out. An organization can make its brand stand out by improving the logo, colors, fonts, packaging, and messaging. If you stand out, you get a larger share of attention and revenues.
Search Engine Optimization	Improving a web page so your target audience can easily find it in search engines.
SEO	See Search Engine Optimization
Spamming a Search Engine	Trying to mislead a search engine to rank your website higher. Don't do this. You'll rank higher for a few days and then you'll be banned.
Target Audience	The target audience is the set of prospects who are likely to be customers of the organization's products and services. You focus your marketing on your target audience. You also save your budget by not marketing at people who aren't in the target audience. In this book, I use "audience," but in marketing, we generally say "target audience" or "TA."
Thank-you Page	The common name for the confirmation page. See Confirmation Page.

Top-line KPIs	At the top of the income statement, the first line (the top line) states the company's total revenues (how much was sold).
Traffic Segmentation	Using analytics to distinguish and compare different audiences. For example, you can segment your web traffic by Google users vs. Yahoo! users and see that Yahoo! users result in 22% more sales.
Unique Selling Proposition (USP)	The unique selling proposition is a short statement that explains why a customer should buy from you instead of your competitors. It states the unique value that you offer, such as an extended warranty, certified service, and so on.
Unique Value Proposition	Another term for USP. See USP.
Unique Visitors	The number of unique visitors who view a web page. A web page may have 100 visitors, but many of them may see the same page several times, so there may be only 60 unique visitors. This doesn't matter very much. Concentrate on conversions.
URI	Unique Resource Identifier. The file name of the item requested by the browser (for example, index.html).
URL	Universal Resource Locator. The address for a website (for example, andreas.com).
URL Tagging	Add a tracking tag to the URL to track activity. For example, in the URL andreas.com/c-m/resources.html/?source=google& medium=ppc& term=book, the URL tag starts after the "/?" and tells us the source is Google, the medium is PPC, and the keyword is book. This information is used by analytics.
Web Analytics	Tools that analyze and compare customer activity in order to make business decisions and increase sales. Analytics tools can report the number of conversions, the keywords that brought conversions, the sites that sent converting traffic, conversion by campaign, and so on.
White paper	A white paper is a corporate name for an expert report. White papers cover general issues for the organization or its products and services. They describe the state of the situation and often include evaluations, recommendations, and forecasts. These tend to be 40-50 pages and written by the organization's experts.

Index

W

X

Y

Z